REPORTS *of* REVIVAL

and

EVANGELISM

from

AFRICA

by

Leroy Hassler

HASSLER EVANGELISTIC MINISTRIES

Library of Congress Control Number:
2021920465

ISBN: 978-0-9719174-1-5

Scripture taken from the King James Version
of the Holy Bible

Photo Cover Credit: Shutterstock.com / Africa continent

Photo Interior Art Credit: Etsy.com / Designesque:
Africa SVG Silhouette w/Madagascar

HASSLER EVANGELISTIC MINISTRIES, INC.®
P. O. Box 1791
Gladewater, TX 75647 USA
www.hasslerministries.com

Book designed and edited by:
S-Y-D Publications®
a publishing ministry of
His Abounding Grace Ministries, Inc.®
McKinney, TX

Printed in the USA by
Morris Publishing®
3212 E. Hwy. 30
Kearney, NE 68847
www.morrispublishing.com

DEDICATION

This book is dedicated to my wonderful wife who has helped and stood behind me and the work all these 50 plus years. She is the finest person I know.

Leroy & Ann 2012

CONTENTS

ACKNOWLEDGEMENTS

I am extremely grateful to my editor Johnnie R. Jones of S-Y-D Publications and His Abounding Grace Ministries, Inc. His guidance, experience, and friendship were valuable in bringing this book to fruition. Also, he exercised a great deal of patience, as this has been a slow project due to a number of reasons.

I never could thank my wife enough for all these great years we have had together and the highly valuable assistance she has been to our ministry and me. She is a great person and I am highly blessed to have her. Every day is a day we enjoy being together.

Many of the acknowledgments are to friends who have encouraged me through the many years and I am thankful for every one of them. If you are already mentioned in the book, it may not be in this list below. No doubt I have failed to mention some that should have been named: Charles Bachtell, Mike Silver, Jerry Morris, Bobby Anderson, John Booker, Ken Rawson, Mike Burns, Mitchell Fortner, Dr. Mike Barnett, Kirby Bozeman, Tim Cannon, George Cammack, Dr. William Duke, Dr. Jimmy Draper, J. R. Duke, Mike Fitzhugh, Marion Fowler, Lindsey Gathright, Don Hayhurst, W. H. Harbour, Larry Hayes, James R. Jones, Alva

Lambert, Carl McInnis, Carter Moore, Foster Mays, Franklin Orr, Bob Patterson, Bill Pratt, Steve Roberson, Ralph Ritzma, Rayford Riley, Dr. Robert Sansom, Chilton Stuart. Bill Thomson, Joseph Tucker, John Thompson, John Toelle, Johnny Upton, Dr. Laney Johnson, Bobby Malone, Robert Smith, Kelly Blomdahl. Tim Sizemore, Herschel Sizemore, Roger Tarver, Chris Moore, Richard Harvey, Glenn Sellers, Jeff Thomas, Jim Parker, Pete Jones, Ed Hulsey, Steve Golden, Bob Fagan, Ken Davis, Daniel Bentley, and Jon Moore.

FOREWORD 1

Preacher, Evangelist, Pastor, Friend, Prayer Warrior, Missionary, and Revivalist is how many of us know Leroy Hassler. By the grace of God, Leroy has been instrumental in providing an example to so many of us in each of these areas. Whether it has been on the dusty roads of Africa, the pulpit of one of our local churches In America, or the office of a friend, Leroy has been a model to all of us as he has sought to honor our Lord in sharing the gospel.

Billy Duncan

It has been my privilege on numerous occasions to have Leroy at the churches I have served and enjoy the rich preaching, and the passion of hearing him share the gospel. When Leroy came to the Lord in the early seventies, the Lord set a fire in his soul that has burned continuously for our Lord. I have always been amazed and yet challenged by his life and commitment. His worldwide ministry has touched the life of uncounted thousands and only eternity will reveal the full impact of his life.

These pages before you will reveal only part of the story of a man who loves the Lord and has served our Lord faithfully.

May the pages of this book stir you and me to greater faith, and may the Lord use them to help us all come to a greater understanding of how the gospel changed one man and sent him on a mission so that many could come to faith in Christ through his preaching and sharing. May the Lord Jesus be exalted and honored in your life through this rich work of my friend, Leroy Hassler.

Billy F. Duncan
Pastor, Beallwood Baptist Church
Columbus, Georgia

FOREWORD 2

One thing I love about being in the battle of expelling darkness and extending the Kingdom of God are the testimonies of God's children. Within the pages of this book, you will find that Ephesians 3:20-21 is fulfilled.... that God is " able to do far more abundantly than all that we ask or think, according to the power at work within us. The following testi-

Dr. Jimmy Blanton

monies will encourage you to remain faithful in the task to which God has called you. There is no doubt that as you hear these testimonies you will see that God is using Brother Leroy as an instrument in His hand to do "far more" than anyone could have expected. God still moves today just as He has always moved. Enjoy the journey as you walk through these pages.

Dr. Jimmy Blanton
Associational Missionary for the Columbus Baptist Association, Columbus, Ga

A Word from My Editor, Johnnie Jones

Back in 2004, when we published Leroy's first book, **The Kind of Preacher God Can Use in God-sent Revival**, I believed this book would become a catalyst to a great awakening and revival throughout the English-speaking world. Each chapter was written from a burdened heart and from someone who had preached thousands of revival messages. Leroy's experiences and life are the kind that God has used time and time again in bringing the lost to Christ. I thought to myself that this book cannot be topped by any other.

Then Leroy asked me to publish another book, **GO! Obeying God in World Evangelism and Revival**. It was released in 2010 and, once again, Leroy shared his heart as to how God burdened him to win 2 million souls to Christ across our globe. At first, I wondered if he could personally accomplish such a ministry. But God showed me that nothing is impossible through a surrendered heart and bold faith to obey Him. And that is what God found in Leroy Hassler. Leroy began circling the globe, preaching the Gospel. It took a few years, but over 2 million souls were recorded as saved, while God honored the prayers, faith, and sacrifices of Leroy and his wife, Ann.

Leroy's third book to be released in early 2022.

But 2 million souls saved was not the end of Leroy's worldwide ministry. While in Africa, God began expanding the work of **Hassler Evangelistic Ministries**. Dozens of churches were planted in numerous African nations, food and Bibles were distributed, and more ministers would join with Leroy and catch their own vision of winning thousands to Christ weekly—sometimes daily! These testimonies come from average folks from many walks of life and are a great portion of Leroy's third book, **Reports of Revival and Evangelism from Africa**, scheduled to be released in 2022.

From these pages, you will discover how Leroy and Ann surrendered their lives to the Lordship of Jesus Christ in southern Alabama and left a successful career in construction work, answering the call of God to be an evangelist. You will follow them to the Dallas area metroplex where I met Leroy at Dallas Baptist University in the mid-seventies. Each page reveals how Leroy and Ann developed a lifestyle of dependency on God's power to accomplish great and mighty works. Together, they demonstrated a life of prayer and faith that caused the hand of God to bring in a tremendous harvest of souls.

Leroy would be the first to say that what he has accomplished was all to the Glory of God. It was God that gave Leroy the vision of reaching 2 million souls to Christ across all the major continents of the world. This number became a catalyst that led many others to follow Leroy into the depths of Africa and proclaim the Gospel. Today, the combined ministries and support of hundreds of people will soon triple Leroy's original number of souls won through **Hassler Evangelistic Ministries**. This third book reveals many testimonies of God at work through his and other ministries that Leroy supports.

Leroy's chapters on prayer and revival will amaze and humble you as you see what God can do through prayer and a humble and surrendered couple such as Leroy and Ann. As you read, you will relive the testimonies of many people who have shared their stories of meeting Leroy and joining him in his burden to win souls to Jesus Christ. Several reoccurring statements in these testimonies are about Leroy's humility and yet how strong he was in sharing the Gospel in remote villages of Africa. Some share how their days were from 12-to-16-plus hours of spreading the Gospel. Some of the testimonies are from the USA, where Leroy shared the Gospel with an old friend or a friend of someone who called Leroy to come share the Gospel.

Reports of Revival and Evangelism from Africa is more than a book of numbers of people being saved and new churches planted. It is, by far, a book demonstrating the ongoing power of God in our current dark and lost world. It is a book that calls out with an invitation to anyone who reads these pages, "Whom shall I send, and who will go for us?" (Isaiah 6:8) I believe God continues to call out those who read Leroy's books and believe in the present power of God to win the lost to Christ. And, best of all, God provides examples in these pages, showing you the ability of joining the ranks of those leading thousands—even millions!—to Christ. Who will God send? One couple, Leroy and Ann Hassler, prayed and said, as Isaiah said, "Here am I; send me!" (6:8)

TESTIMONIES FROM THOSE WHO HAVE TRAVELED WITH LEROY HASSLER OR SERVE HASSLER EVANGELISTIC MINISTRIES

INTRODUCTION – WHAT GOD IS DOING IN AFRICA

By Leroy Hassler

I am often asked how we reach so many people for Christ. The answer is in the following pages. Do not forget about the power of God. All Glory to God! The people are out there, we do not wait for them to come to us; we go to where they are.

We preach in schools, colleges, and universities. We have a wide-open door in much of Africa to preach the gospel in an uncompromising manner and give an invitation for people to pray to receive Christ as Lord and Savior. We have now preached in 4,000 plus schools. I have personally preached to over 10,000 students before lunch in India.

We have preached in schools in Africa, India, Europe, and North and Central America.

A 12-hour, and many times, over an 18-hour workday and more are considered normal workdays by this ministry.

17

THE JESUS FILM – is the number one tool for reaching people who have not been reached for Christ. We have done thousands of Jesus Films with the gospel being preached at the end and an invitation given for people to receive Christ. This film is based on the life of Christ from the gospel of Luke. It goes from the birth of Christ through his life, death, burial and resurrection.

We have seen people walk for miles to see a 2-hour long film then stand for another half hour for the message and invitation. Sometimes hundreds come and often many times thousands come. We have seen as many as 10,000 to 15,000 come to the film and completely block the roads and traffic. The film is in the language of the people. We have run 6 films a night in many locations drawing out thousands to see the film and hear the message. We now help finance the showing of over 100 films a month that many thousands come to see.

One African man asked me, "How is it that Jesus speaks our language?"

We have started over 400 new Churches mostly in Africa. We always have local pastors at the Jesus Film to do counseling with those making decisions for Christ. They take many of the people who made decisions at the Jesus Film and start new churches with the new converts. We also preach in churches on Sundays.

By God's grace we have done discipleship training and many pastor conferences where pastors receive training and spiritual help.

We have given away thousands of Bibles in Africa and many thousands of Bibles in China.

We give financial support to missionaries and pastors in Africa, India, Europe, Mexico, Central America, and South America.

How is it that so many decisions for Christ are made? First all Glory to God for every decision. He gets the credit. Sometimes we report only what our ministry accomplishes. But sometimes we report joint efforts for Christ by one or two additional ministries that this ministry helped start and heavily financed. They operate exactly the same way as our ministry.

THE FOLLOWING SECTION OF TESTIMONIES ARE FROM MINISTERS AND LAYPEOPLE WHO HAVE GONE WITH ME TO AFRICA.

WEST AFRICA – 1997

"But with God all things are possible!" Matthew 19:26

TESTIMONY FROM A SENIOR ADULT

Next to the day I got saved, the trip to Africa with Leroy Hassler was the most exciting adventure of my life of nearly 68 years. Never in my life have I seen so many thousands of people give their lives to Christ. When Leroy Hassler finished preaching, I saw the young, the old, and people from all walks of life, come forward during the

Lamar Hearn
1929-2021

19

invitation to give their lives totally to Christ. Leroy preached the gospel in an uncompromising manner, whether the crowd was ten, or more than ten thousand. To him, each person is important to reach for our Lord. Ghana has great needs and we experienced them during the hundreds of miles we traveled.

When Leroy invited me to go to Ghana, West Africa, with him last fall, I did not know what to expect. Many surprises were in store for me. The first thing was the beauty of Ghana. I have been to Hawaii, yet I saw Ghana as being far more beautiful with its bright green foliage and fruit of every kind growing everywhere. The second surprise was the friendly people. The people of Ghana are the kindest people I have met anywhere in the world, and I have traveled extensively.

A third surprise was the amazing openness of the people to the gospel. I saw more people come to Christ in sixteen days, than I had in the past sixty-eight years I have been alive. Leroy Hassler is taking the gospel into places that Dr. Billy Graham and others will never be able to go. He is taking the gospel into places with no electricity, no television, and no radio. He is going into big cities, the little cities, villages, and to remote tribal people. Even some of the African people cannot keep up with the pace he sets in getting the gospel out.

Enduring the heat and sleeping in a hotel room with rats, was worth it, to see over 27,000 people come to Christ! I thank God he let me live long enough to see a real miracle.[1]

– Lamar Hearn from Smith, Alabama

[1]The above was taken from the book, **GO! Obeying God in World Evangelism** by Leroy Hassler

NEIL KOON

During the week of April 8, 1979, Leroy Hassler was preaching a revival at Concord Baptist Church in Bleecker, Alabama. My brother, Irvin Koon, had lung cancer and asked Leroy to visit him. Irvin asked Leroy and me if God was going to heal him or if he was going to die. Leroy earnestly prayed for him during the visit and continued praying through the night.

The next day (I believe it was the 10th or 11th of April), Leroy told me that the Lord had told him that He wasn't going to heal Irvin. I told Irvin what the Lord had revealed to Leroy. Irvin died a few days later, on April 13, 1979.

Irvin knew the Lord could heal because he had experienced healing from the Lord just ten years earlier. In 1969, Irvin had been hospitalized and near the point of death from cirrhosis of the liver due to alcoholism. The Doctor told Irvin to "get his business in order" because he didn't have long to live.

The men of Concord Church, led by pastor James Mooney, prayed earnestly for Irvin during that time. Irvin made a full recovery and completely stopped drinking. The Lord delivered him from alcoholism and death.

In the 1950's, Neil, Irvin, and their Dad were in the woods sawmilling. During a lunch break, Irvin asked Neil and their Dad if they wanted to know ahead of time when they were going to die. Irvin's Dad replied, "It doesn't matter to me. I will be ok with the Lord if I die instantly." (Irvin's Dad died instantly of a heart attack, July 4, 1962). Neil replied, "I don't want to say, I want the Lord to handle my leaving here." (Neil is 93 years old now). Irvin said, "I want to know ahead of time." Through Leroy, the Lord let Irvin know before he died on April 13, 1979.

Neil Koon
October 12, 2020

A Note from Leroy Hassler – I met Neil Koon and his wife and family during the very first revival meeting I preached in 1974 at Concord Baptist Church in Bleecker, Alabama. Neil's wonderful Christian wife, Grace, went to be with the Lord a short time ago. I met many people in that revival that became lifelong friends, like Lamar Hearn, Bill and Charlotte Ashcraft, Rev. & Mrs. James Mooney, who was the pastor and his wife. These wonderful friends have all gone on to be with the Lord. I also met Jonathan and Mary Jane, Neil and Grace's fine son and daughter.

The entire Koon family is more than just our casual friends. They have spent time in our home in Texas and we have spent time in their home that is near the Alabama/Georgia state line. Mary Jane's husband, Jerry Rudd, went to Malawi with me and did an excellent job. I have no idea of how many meals Neil and I have had together through these more than 47 plus years now. Neil has attended many revival meetings in two states in which I preached.

For many years Neil had a prayer meeting for genuine revival, in his office in Phenix City, Alabama. I have driven over 100 miles, a number of times, to attend. It is one of the most spiritual prayer meetings I have ever attended. Brother

Neil has a deep walk with the Lord and has maintained it for many years now.

MALAWI, AFRICA 2007

LEROY HASSLER, BILL LANGLEY, DR. ROSS COLLIER (IMB Missionary), JERRY RUDD, BUD PASSMORE, & DR. WILLIAM DUKE

MALAWI – 2007

*Not by might, nor by power, but by my spirit,
saith the Lord of hosts.* –Zechariah 4:6

One of the six men who went with me to Malawi was Bill Langley from Flint, Texas near Tyler. Bill and I preached to about 60,000 people, in nine days. Brother Bill said, "What Brother Hassler said came true, because I saw more people come to Christ than I had in all the many years of my ministry put together! All this happened in less than 2 weeks. The people of Malawi were more open to the gospel than I ever dreamed."

Bill did an extraordinary job, considering this was his first trip to Africa. He preached to four thousand, or more each night.

The large crowds can be overwhelming, even to an experienced preacher; plus the work is very fast-paced. Once in West Africa one of our preachers could not keep up the pace and asked to be put on a plane back to his home in America. Although he was past sixty-five, Bill kept a very tough schedule that would burn out some preachers half his age. (Preachers preach in schools in the daytime and at the Jesus Film at night. We had 6 Jesus films going at night in many locations. They also may preach in churches on Sunday and at a pastor conference. This involves many miles of travel. Sometimes over 100 miles a day.)[1]

Bill Langley and his wife Wanda are members of Green Acres Baptist Church in Tyler, Texas. For a number of years, he taught a large Sunday school class there. He gave me the privilege of sharing about our ministry with the class on several occasions. Bill is a retired pastor.

[1] The above first 2 paragraphs were taken from the book **GO! Obeying God in World Evangelism** by Leroy Hassler.

TESTIMONY FROM A NORTH CAROLINA PASTOR

Rev. David E. "Eddy" Driver, Pastor
Charity Baptist Church, Boonville, NC

Dear Bro. Leroy,
I would like to thank you for the invitation given to join you in the work of the Lord in Zambia. But even more so, I would like to praise the Lord for placing me upon your heart. I realize that God could have used anyone to do  what He used me to do in Zambia, but according to His good

pleasure, He chose to allow someone like me to be a part of His great work for which I am truly grateful.

He truly is doing a great work within the large areas of Africa, but it is truly amazing what we witnessed Him do in Kitwe and other parts of Zambia. It is rare to see such a hunger for the word of God! Simple evangelistic messages were preached to the people with a tremendous response. It reminds me of the early days of the church in which the Lord added hundreds and thousands to the church daily. I mean we would preach to groups of 2,000 - 3,000 and sometimes more (300 to 500 was a small group!) and almost everyone present would respond at the invitation by lifting their hand for salvation. I truly have never seen nothing like it! It was people of all ages. Some would be so anxious to come to Christ they would not wait until the Jesus Film for the commitment card but would come immediately asking for the card to be filled out. It was an absolute preacher's paradise in the sense that every time that I preached (except one) people were making decisions - people were giving their hearts to the Lord! God is truly doing a great work in Zambia, and He is doing a great work through Hassler Evangelistic Ministries.

The hunger for the Word of God could also be seen by the many requests that we had for Bibles. Though we were able to distribute some Bibles, and most of them to the schools we visited, we could have given away many times more if we just had them to give. What a blessing it would be should the Lord impress His people to give in order that many more Bibles could be purchased to give to the people. It is my prayer that everyone who desires a Bible for the purpose of growing in the Lord would be provided with one. I would also like to thank the Lord for our African brothers that are committed to this: getting the word of God to the people and providing the people with the New Testament in Bemba as well as Chochewee. But they also lack resources. What a shame! There are so many Bibles in the United States that lay around for weeks or months collecting dust while there are thousands upon thousands of people in Zambia that are longing to get just one Bible in their possession. May God have mercy on us! And may He continue to use us to get the Word to the people through preaching as well as getting more Bibles into their hands.

Thank you again brother for the invitation to go and be part of this great work of the Lord. It was an honor and privilege. Perhaps the Lord will open the door for me to join you again in this great work. I hope so! But most of all, I praise the Lord for what He is doing in Zambia. I praise Him for every heart that has been won to Him for His honor and glory. I praise Him for every seed that has been sown in His name and pray that it will bring forth the fruit of salvation. And I praise Him for allowing this preacher the great honor of sharing Jesus with those who are so spiritually hungry in Zambia. I had better go for now. God bless you, your ministry, and your wonderful wife.[1]

[1]Eddy went to Zambia several times with our ministry and went to Malawi.

TESTIMONY FROM A VETERINARIAN

Dear Leroy,

Words cannot express the gratitude that I have by being able to go to Malawi in order to preach the Gospel of Jesus Christ. Next to my salvation and marriage to my

Dr. William Duke
Dothan, AL

wonderful wife, Elizabeth, this was the best experience I have ever had. God was able to crush my heart and use me as an instrument for His eternal purpose. To God be the Glory! The harvest in Malawi is abundant, but the laborers are few. The number of souls reached was only hindered by the time we had to preach.

Many things happened in Malawi that would seem bizarre here in the USA. In one instance I was preaching a Sunday morning church service. This was the first church service that I had ever preached. We were starting a church in the village that I was preaching and there was no building. The service was much longer than what we would have in America. I was the third person to preach and that was after Sunday School and much singing. It was extremely hot, and the women and children all sat underneath a group of low-limbed trees. Not even five minutes into my message a green mamba (Africa's deadliest snake) dropped out of the trees among the women and children. All I witnessed was a lot of screaming and running followed by a very fast-moving green snake traveling in front of me. Before you could think, a man wearing just sandals stomped on the snake's head, killing it in an instant. There is no sitting on the fence in Malawi. Hesitation will get you killed.

When the service resumed, I told the women that God must have seen them sleeping and wanted to wake them up! There are many other stories that I could tell, and I am sure everyone came away from the trip with a bunch of memories. I would recommend this trip to everyone that can go. It was a great blessing to me and continues to bless me even now.[1]

[1]Dr. Duke went to Malawi several times and Zambia with our ministry.

MY EXPERIENCES IN ZAMBIA

Leroy Hassler, Ed Hulsey, Jerry Richie, Jim Kisner Kenneth Bowden, and the African Team

Zambia May 2005

Like so many people today, I thought I was doing just fine as a Christian by attending my church, paying tithe, and trying each day to do the right thing and treat people with respect. All those are good things and to be applauded, but I find that to be not only the "minimum" we owe God for what he has done for us. There is much more we owe Him for what Jesus has sacrificed.

When my wife and I moved to Longview, Texas from California in 1995, we joined Moberly Baptist church almost immediately. We also started a rental business by purchasing old houses and renovating them to rent out to people and reap some positive cash flow. The business was going well, and we soon met Leroy Hassler and discovered what he was doing in his worldwide ministry. We discovered he was traveling to many parts of the world where the living conditions would be considered far below the poverty line here in the US. I knew that his ministry was a worthwhile cause, so Shirley and I decided we need to support a ministry like that. In 1997, we made our first monthly contribution to Hassler Evangelistic Ministries; it was $25 dollars. The business was just getting underway, and the cash flow was not significant, but we knew God would make our contributions more efficient for His purposes. It has been more than 20 years since that first contribution and the Lord has prospered us to be able to increase that amount significantly.

For many years I looked at the culture here in America and what I saw was beautiful churches on nearly every corner in our towns and cities. We have air-conditioned buildings, padded seats, big parking lots, wonderful pastors and speakers, sound systems, video systems, help for the hearing impaired, beautiful Christmas pageants, lots of room for small group studies, and free Bibles if you want them.

Of course, to pay for all this, the costs are high. There are electric bills to pay, gas and water bills as well. Then there are the gardeners and the church staff to pay. Also, there is maintenance of the building and grounds. Insurance is not cheap and other costs abound that I have not even considered but they do exist. The result is that about 10% of all the money brought in goes to missions or some other spiritual endeavor, while all the rest goes to keep the doors open. To make matters worse, the membership is barely enough to pay those expenses and the population at large sees no need of joining a church. The problem, of course, is that we in America have been blessed with so much that we think it is our own endeavors that made it that way. We have become complacent. We have become self-sufficient! As a country, we are prideful. The first crisis that hits our country brings people back to the church until the crisis is over and the newcomers then go back to "business as usual." I don't feel sorry for my countrymen, but at the same time, I pray that as a country we will come back to our roots and put Jesus back in charge.

This is why Shirley and I decided to support Leroy Hassler. Up to that point I never experienced what people go through in third-world countries. I only saw it on television programs but being there is a whole new experience. In 2005 Leroy asked me to go to Zambia, Africa with him to minister to the people. I was a little nervous about preaching to a large crowd, but Leroy told me to keep it simple. When we landed in Lusaka, Zambia, we went to the hotel and unpacked. The next day we were taken to a school of about 1500 elementary children. Leroy gave the message with an interpreter and at least 1000 children gave their hearts to Christ. I was shocked and amazed at the response. In America, we would be glad to get five people from a crowd that size. The preaching continued for ten days, and thousands responded to the gospel. I received my first chance to speak to crowds of kids about the third day. I was nervous, but the message was received with gladness and hundreds came to Christ. I cannot tell you the feeling of gratitude the Lord gave me for the opportunity to speak truth to people that are hungry for the news of Jesus.

In Zambia, many people have one meal a day and many others don't get that. The houses that people lived in would be the equivalent of a storage shed in America. You were lucky if you had a job and if you did, you were supporting a large family because many relatives died early in life and their family came to live with you. Others, not as lucky, lived on the streets or under a makeshift shelter with no walls. But when they heard of Christ, and their eternal home, they knew there was hope. Bibles are in short supply and many people had nothing more than a couple of pages ripped out of a Bible that they shared with others; then traded their pages for pages from other people.

On the way to one of the villages, I noticed several burned fields. I asked the interpreter why so many burned areas. I was told that many of the people in the country set the fields on fire to capture the rabbits and rodents for food as they scurried from their hiding places. When we arrived at our destination, I was scheduled to preach to a village of about 100 people. We had plenty of time before starting, so I was talking to a village woman who indicated they wanted to build a church. The current church was a thatched hut with no walls and a bunch of weeds and grass woven together for a roof. That was when the Spirit convicted me to do something about it. I prayed with the people that night before showing the Jesus film and told them if they really believed, they would have their new church building. Leaving that village, I knew what the Lord was asking me to do. It wasn't too long before doubt came to me about what I knew God was asking me to accomplish, but I prayed for assurance and God delivered. I asked my church small group to support that cause and as many people prayed, the money came in. One person received a thousand-dollar bonus at work and gave the whole amount to the cause. After three months passed, more than $4000 dollars was raised and sent to Hassler Ministries to build that church. I was very blessed to be in Zambia two years later to go back to that village and preach in that church to celebrate what God could do if we had enough faith.

One of the high schools I visited on the last day there that year made an impression on me I will never forget. After giving the message to the students, I asked them if they had any

Jim Kisner with members of a new church he helped start in 2005.

questions for me. Although none of the students had questions, one of the administrators said he had a question. His question was, "America has done so much to help countries like ours, what could we do to help America?" I was stunned at that question for a few moments, but the Holy Spirit gave me the answer. I told him, "Come to America and give us the gospel." He was stunned at my answer because he said America is a Christian nation. To which I responded, "We are rapidly becoming a godless nation and Christians are now a minority." I knew if many Americans could see the happiness on the faces of Africans who knew Christ, it would make an impact; especially on those who sit in our pews and go through the rituals as if to think to themselves, "Well, here I am...feed me."

There is no doubt in my mind that at this very moment my wife, Shirley, who has passed on in January 2020, is talking to Africans who are thanking her that she had sent the funds to help bring them to Christ through the messages of Hassler Ministries. I look forward to meeting those brothers and sisters in Christ and wrapping my arms around them and telling them, "We were only doing our duty, the glory goes to Jesus who made it all possible."

Jim Kisner
Brother in Christ

THE HIGHLIGHTS OF THE WORK DONE IN ZAMBIA THROUGH HASSLER EVANGELISTIC MINISTRIES INTERNATIONAL

By Rev. Frawell Chipata

Hassler Evangelistic Ministries International (H.E.M.I.) is an evangelistic ministry whose core purpose is to bring people in the fear of God: by proclaiming the word of God to the lost and to make known of our salvation through Christ our Lord. H.E.M.I. has been reaching out with the good news since 2003. Since its inception, the Ministry has been successfully progressing in that the message has been conveyed to over one million people.

An overwhelming response from people and students has been seen. The H.E.M.I. focus is on four areas:

➢   Preaching the gospel to the lost together with students;

➢   Discipling new believers;

➢   Reaching out and supporting the new disciples with materials, such as Bibles, soccer balls, etc.; and,

➢   Starting new churches.

In 2003, we started in Lusaka (capital city of Zambia), 10 night crusades using Jesus film were conducted and 46 schools that included secondary and primary schools were reached.

In 2004, we went to Livingstone (the tourist capital of Zambia located in the Southern Province) where we saw 9 night crusades involving 39 schools. These schools included both secondary and primary schools.

In 2005, we came back to Lusaka and 36 night crusades using four (4) teams were conducted and 60 schools, both secondary and primary, were reached.

In 2006, we went to the city of Kitwe on the Copperbelt province of Zambia and we had 30 night crusades using three (3) teams and 38 schools, both secondary and primary were ministered to.

In 2007, for the first time, we went to Lilongwe, the capital city of Malawi, where 36 night crusades were conducted and 56 schools, both primary and secondary, were ministered to.

In 2008, we went to Mazabuka, a town in the Southern province of Zambia, with three (3) teams and 24 night crusades were conducted and 32 schools were ministered to.

In 2009, two teams went to Kabwe the provincial headquarters of Central Province of Zambia and 18 night crusades were conducted and targeted 32 schools.

In 2010, we returned to Lusaka (the capital city of Zambia). Four (4) teams managed to conduct 36 night crusades and 60 schools were reached.

In 2011, in Ndola, the provincial headquarters of the Copperbelt province, three (3) teams successfully undertook 24 night crusades and 34 schools were reached.

In 2012, we went to Kabwe again and a total of 17 night crusades were conducted and 22 schools were ministered to.

In 2013, two teams went to Chongwe, a rural town on the east of Lusaka, where 16 night crusades were conducted and 25 schools were ministered to.

In 2014, we were graced with the presence of Rev. Ken Rawson and together we created three (3) teams that conducted 24 crusades in Lusaka and 48 schools were ministered to.

In 2015, four (4) teams embarked on a mission to Chipata the provincial headquarters of Eastern province of Zambia. The mission was to conduct 36 night crusades and I am pleased to inform you that it was a success as 48 schools were ministered to.

In 2016, our two (2) teams conducted 16 night crusades and 23 schools were ministered to. These were locally conducted.

Leroy Hassler and Frawell Chipata

In 2017 we were again honored with the presence of Rev. Ken Rawson and together we created two (2) teams and conducted 19 night crusades and 27 schools were ministered to.

These are the highlights of the work done in Zambia through the Hassler Evangelistic Ministries International and I am pleased to inform you that we recorded great success in most of our evangelistic ventures. Churches, schools, and people also benefited so much from the activities of Brother Hassler's ministry.

For more details or clarity on any of our activities highlighted herein, kindly contact me. You may also seek clarity on any of our activities that may not have been highlighted in the summarized report.

Thank you and may our God continue blessing you.

REV. FRAWELL CHIPATA

MY EXPERIENCE WITH HASSLER MINISTRIES IN AFRICA

By Jerry Rudd, Phenix City, Alabama

On my trip to Malawi, I had the opportunity to share the Gospel in many schools where the students were very receptive to the words of Christi,

MALAWI, AFRICA 2007

LEROY HASSLER, BILL LANGLEY, DR. ROSS COLLIER (IMB Missionary), JERRY RUDD, BUD PASSMORE, & DR. WILLIAM DUKE

unlike American schools where we are not able to share and preach. I was able to share the Gospel in 10 schools and over 10,000 decisions were made to follow Christ. One elementary school in particular, an orphanage school, whose parents had passed away from AIDS, made an impact on me. The children were happy, smiling and did not seem to have a care in the world, although I was told that most of the children would not live to be 15 years of age. Through the sharing of Christ with these children, their souls will live on in heaven.

I also had the opportunity to preach at the Senior Pastor's church on Sunday. Since I am not a preacher by trade, it can be difficult to share the gospel through an interpreter. (Proper English and South Alabama English do not translate very well.) None the less, it was a very productive service, as 17 people received Christ that day.

We as Americans look at people we consider poverty stricken as unintelligent, lazy, and unwilling to work to better themselves. We cannot compare America to other countries, especially what Americans would consider third world countries. Most of the people in Malawi and other third world counties are doing the best they can, they are not dumb. They are actually very ingenious and make the best of what they have.

There is a lot of work still to be done, because not only are Christian organizations sharing the gospel in these countries, but also, Muslim, Hindu and other false doctrines are being shared as well. When I walk the streets of Heaven, I look forward to walking beside some of these beautiful people that I had the great opportunity to meet.

MY TRIP TO LUSAKA, AFRICA, WITH HASSLER MINISTRIES

By Pastor David Baxley, D. Min.

It was my privilege to be able to take a mission trip to Lusaka Zambia, in south Africa, with Bro. Leroy and several others in March of 2006. The thing that stands out most to me was the hunger for the gospel. People would walk for miles and stand for long periods of time just to hear about Jesus. It was not a vacation because we worked hard every day. We

Dr. David Baxley & Charles Harvey

would go into the school and were given the opportunity to share Jesus with the students. On visit to a local school the head mistress told the children to listen carefully because this would be the most important lesson they would receive today. They allowed an invitation after the message and many children came to know Christ. In the evenings we would drive to a vacant lot in town set up a screen and show the Jesus movie, where hundreds would come to receive Christ.

Brother Leroy Hassler has the mission churches and mission work very well organized to be most effective and is not afraid to spend the money necessary to reach people for Christ, but is a very good steward over how it is spent. God has very richly blessed the mission efforts in Zambia and Brother Hassler's work with the native pastors and workers.

MISSION TRIPS TO AFRICA WITH HASSLER MINISTRIES

By Tom L. Anderson, Retired Pastor, Dothan, Alabama

Leroy Hassler, Eugene Narth, and Tom Anderson in Mankessim, Ghana

Introduction by Leroy Hassler – We have known Tom and his wife, Irene, since early 1973. Tom knocked on my door in Dothan, Alabama and invited us to church. Later I went to Baptist Bible Institute at Graceville, Florida, with Tom. The Andersons are wonderful friends and great people.

Our days at Cloverdale Baptist Church in Dothan were great God filled days. We had Henry Johnson as a pastor and friend.

Tom has since been the pastor of churches in Georgia and Alabama.

Testimony by Tom Anderson – I want to share what Brother Leroy Hassler's ministry has meant to me. I met him in 1973. He was a welding inspector at the nuclear plant in Houston County, Alabama, and God touched his heart and gave him a great desire to see lost people saved. And most of them were outside of the United States.

Leroy Hassler with his welding truck and rig on a pipeline south of Birmingham, Alabama. Leroy worked on many construction jobs as a welder, pipe fabricator, foreman, and superintendent. He left the construction work after being called to preach on April 7, 1974.

I had opportunity to go with Leroy and his ministry into Africa on three occasions over 20 years ago. I can absolutely say it was a highlight of my life to see God work in a way that was similar to the book of Acts. Each of those three weeks, I would preach to over 25,000 people, the simple, powerful gospel of the Bible. Each of those weeks, I would see approximately 15,000 people make decisions to put their faith in Jesus Christ. You see, that would be 45,000 people. It caused me to realize that in the

United States of America, in our effort to help the gospel, we may have actually hindered it.

Leroy, I don't know what you'll do with this testimony, but I do thank God for you, your vision, and your love for lost people. I count it an honor to consider you as my brother and one of my best friends.

Bro. Tom Anderson

AFRICAN ADVENTURES WITH HASSLER MINISTRIES

By Jerry Richie, Longview, Texas

MAZABUKA, ZAMBIA CRUSADE – MAY 2008
Team Leaders, 2 American & 2 African

LEROY HASSLER, OSCAR, CHRIS, & JERRY RICHIE

My African adventures all started in 2004 when one day at church, Brother Leroy Hassler struck up a conversation with me about some of his missionary experiences in Africa. Before then I had not even thought about going there for any reason. During the conversation he asked if I'd like to go with him sometime. I said I would think about it. Soon after that, he gave me a book about the life of Dr. David Livingstone and how he blazed the trail in Africa for other missionaries. After much prayer, I decided to go, but only as an observer. Up until that time, I had only led one person to Christ and that was my young daughter, so I was not prepared to do anything like that in Africa.

As we all know, our plans are not always God's plans. One morning as we were waiting outside in front of our hotel in Livingstone, Zambia, Pastor Paul Stewart noticed a young man standing on the sidewalk several feet away. Paul said, "I'm going to go talk to that young man." We all knew that meant he was going to share the gospel with him. A few minutes later, Paul returned with a big smile on his face indicating that the man had accepted Christ! After a brief time of rejoicing, Paul saw another young man close by. He then turned to me and said, "Now it's your turn." I'll never forget those words, nor will I ever forget the boldness that I felt from the Holy Spirit in that moment as I walked up to that young man and shared the plan of salvation with him. He became the second person I had ever led to the Lord.

We later visited many African schools, visited several villages, showing the Jesus film, and led many people to Christ.

Since then, I have made five other trips to Africa and have been used by the Holy Spirit to lead hundreds—maybe thousands—of people to Jesus. Thank you, Brother Leroy Hassler, for this opportunity.

ENCOURAGEMENT TO GO ON A MISSION TRIP

Charles Harvey, Retired Minister, Wiggins, Mississippi

Introduction by Leroy Hassler – Unlike most of the people mentioned in the book, except Neil Koon and Tom Anderson, I have known Charles Harvey well over 40 years now. I first met Charles, his wife, Ginny, and their 4 children at a revival meeting in Mobile, Alabama. Charles was the minister of music there and led the music in a marvelous way during the revival that I preached in. The church had been looking for someone to preach a revival meeting and contacted well-

Charles Harvey also preached on many occasions in Africa.

known Alabama evangelist, Junior Hill. Brother Hill already had a revival meeting scheduled on the date but asked them to get Leroy Hassler. So that is how God arranged for me to meet Charles Harvey and his family.

I kept in contact with Charles and his family. Later he became the pastor of a Baptist Church in Mississippi. He invited me to preach a revival meeting there in the early 1980's.

In 1983 I was called to pastor Eastside Baptist Church at Rusk, Texas. A year or two later the church called Charles Harvey to be Minister of Music and Education. As always, he did an extraordinary job. Charles is one of the hardest workers I have even met, and he put his all into the church work there. R. S. Dyess and his wife worked with the youth there and did an excellent job. Esther, his wife, has since gone on to be with the Lord.

God gave me some of the very best people to help me there and that was a great blessing. My wife made countless visits with me on the church field and was a great asset to our ministry.

Testimony by Charles Harvey – As I look back on my mission trips, I feel compelled to encourage those who are following the Holy Spirit's call to participate in mission trips. There are those who are seeking to convert the lost to Jesus Christ. They, as I, want to find their place in mission efforts to convert and to aid the converted in attaining an abundant life in Christ.

As I participated in the Hassler Evangelistic missions to Zambia, a landlocked country in central Africa, I wanted to reach the people by teaching the Bible to their local pastors, reaching into their schools, and using the Jesus films. My desire in Zambia was to work with local Baptist pastors and leaders to introduce real prayer and a true inward experience of Christ as hundreds heard the gospel, the good news of Jesus—His birth, crucifixion, and ascension, desiring converts to go on and become true disciples, giving the Lord their whole heart.

Upon landing in Lusaka, Zambia airport, our Hassler Evangelistic team, led by evangelist Leroy Hassler, met the local pastors who served as guides and translators. They accompanied us to our housing. Our housing compound was adequate with bedrooms and a cafeteria. That was a first time for me to sleep in a bed totally enclosed by netting due to malaria carried by mosquitoes.

The next day I was driven to several schools where I shared the good news of Jesus Christ. After our evening meal, I was driven by my assigned guide to show the Jesus film and give a brief message during the film's intermission. That was our schedule daily. On Sunday, I preached in a local church; my guide was the pastor.

We did have one afternoon for sightseeing. On the last full day, the team led a Bible conference for pastors from surrounding villages.

Looking at the events of the week, I felt somewhat overwhelmed. After a heart-to-heart talk with God, I began each day renewed. As I entered the airport to return home, I honestly felt that I had only been there a couple of days. God renewed me daily, leading me from school to school, preaching, showing the Jesus film, and helping local pastors in Bible studies. I was actually seeing miracle after miracle among the people in Lusaka.

According to Psalm 116:6, we have been assured that the Lord God loves to give Himself to those who need Him. God will work through those who are willing to teach a believer to seek God within his own heart. What a joy to let God work in one's life to reach the lost all over the world. My experiences have been filled with the awesomeness of God's love.

To those considering mission trips, Jesus Christ loves you. He saved you. You love Him. Jesus is calling—listen closely, hear Him calling you to missions... the harvest is ready. Will you go in His name to rescue the lost and lead the converts to their fullness in Christ? Find your joy... I give glory to the holiness of God.

I give my sincere thanks to Leroy Hassler and my fellow team members for their contributions to the Great Commission.

Charles Harvey

CALLED TO MISSIONS
By Nathan Durant

Leroy Hassler and I began a friendship some thirty-five years ago when he preached a revival at Victory Park Baptist Church, McAlester, Oklahoma, where I was a member. Having become a follower of Jesus Christ not so long before this, I absorbed everything he had to say. He told us, "the world needed a lot  of things, but the thing they needed most was Jesus Christ," which the Bible confirms through and through. That's a given now, but I was young and taking in much information about spiritual things.

My spiritual mentor is one who calmly and plainly presents the gospel of Christ. He's not real flashy in his presentation but over and over I have witnessed the spiritual results evident in our church people. They started sharing about Jesus more, many accepting Christ as their Savior, and keeping in contact with us through the years about their continual ministry. Once I received the pastorate, calling Leroy was invited several times to minister in our church. While he could have been preaching doctrinal type messages which can also be valuable, his primary emphasis continued to focus on Jesus Christ and getting Christ to the world.

Although I knew about missionaries, I wasn't exposed to this kind of thinking until I heard Brother Leroy. Then it became a focus of mine. Because of his influence in my life and his decision to stay with the gospel message, I found myself prioritizing that in my ministry through the years. Wherever the Lord moved us, Leroy was always invited to share his wisdom with our congregations, sharing Jesus as the Savior for the world.

Sometime in the 1990s, while Brother Leroy was preaching, the Lord started impressing on me the need to do missions regularly. A short time later, our family started going to Mexico to preach the Good News and eventually on to Nicaragua. What I learned years ago remained true for today, that Jesus was our only way to heaven, and this remains our ministry focus within Like Elijah Ministry. I realize that we've been blessed to be a part of the mission's ministry for close to 17 years and during that time we have preached to thousands, the very same message that brings folks together through salvation. As Leroy mentored me through the years, encouraging me in scriptures, suggesting books to read on becoming a disciple maker, and just by setting an example to be faithful in his walk, I'm following that same path. I've learned to encourage my Spanish brothers in Christ as I was taught.

Because of Leroy's ministry to my family, we have been able to "make disciples of the nations," just as Matthew 28:19-20 instructs us. God bless you, my brother in Christ, as you continue to help others go on missions and share the Gospel of Jesus Christ!

Nathan Durant
Like Elijah Ministry, Inc
P.O. BOX 963
Krebs, OK 74554

EATING ELEPHANT IN ZAMBIA

By Edward Hulsey

Every afternoon was filled with excitement as the Hassler Evangelistic team members prepared to take the Gospel to some primitive villages. We were organized into teams: Hassler team members, local pastors, interpreters, and members of the Hassler Zambia teams.

We never knew how many people to expect or what to expect of the condition of our equipment. Sometimes the equipment didn't work so we spent extra time asking Father God to make it work. Most of the time it did.

Some villages would be nothing but grass-thatched roofs and mud walls. Occasionally there would be a home with electricity. Our routine was simple: find an open spot in the village, set up our movie screen, hook up the projector and wait for it to get dark so that the movie, The Jesus Film, would be visible. Watching a movie and seeing white men was a real treat for the villagers and the outliers around the village. Many of those who showed up to see and hear the movie lingered behind buildings or remained in the darkness, so we never knew the size of our audience. We just knew they were there.

Generally, the initial excitement as we set up for the evening show was by the village children. They wanted to be around us, talk to us, and touch our skin. I think they thought our white would rub off. They were so delightful to be around. But one afternoon as our team pulled into a village, there was a great excitement going on. It didn't take us long to find out the cause of this extra excitement. The village was located close to a natural game reserve. Many wild animals lived in that reserve, especially elephants. Occasionally some of the elephants would wander out of the reserve and pose a threat to villages in the area. This was one of those days.

Normally, the reserve rangers would manage to drive the elephants back home. This day one of the elephants refused to return to the reserve, went rouge and was deemed a threat to the village where we were to set up. Regretfully the rangers had to shoot the elephant to stop him. I say regretfully, because that was how I felt. But the villagers felt differently. An elephant is a lot of meat and there was no reason to let it go to waste. That's how the villagers felt. All the villagers had brought their knives and machetes and began carving up that huge carcass.

They cut that elephant into huge pieces and were hurrying back to their hut to start cooking it. One woman stopped and let us look at the meat. It was very red and lean and appeared to have no fat, a great Sunday roast. I was told that elephant tasted a lot like venison, but figured I would never get to taste it.

Normally the villagers would get a movie and a presentation of the Gospel. This night they got all that but then had a feast of elephant to eat afterwards. They felt blessed as did I. I shall never forget that night, not just because of the elephant dinner, but because I was blessed to present the Gospel of Jesus Christ to some people. Father God has blessed me in so many uncountable ways. I praise Him, exalt Him, and love Him for allowing me to share this story with you.

THE MIRACLE CONVERSION OF MIKE HARTLESS

By Renea Elliot of Carthage, Texas

I know several of you have heard this story, but in case you haven't....

My father, Mike Hartless went to high school with Leroy Hassler in Carthage, Texas. They were friends throughout school, but lost contact after graduation. Dad did not want anything to do with a computer. No email address, no Facebook, nothing. Because of this, he had heard bits and pieces of Mr. Hassler's mission work. Dad had been in bad health for several years. He was a diabetic, had high blood pressure, had a huge hernia that he was refusing to have surgery for, and was having some heart problems. Dad found out he had prostate cancer, but was not a candidate for some treatment options because of his weight. Before doctors could decide how to treat him for cancer, Dad started having congestive heart failure. A neighbor noticed Dad sitting in his truck where he parked his trailers and equipment. About an hour later the neighbor passed by again and saw that Dad was still sitting in the same spot.

If any of you knew my father, then you know that this was not like him. He was usually on the move. The neighbor called my mom and she went to check on him. She questioned him about being so swollen and he admitted that he wasn't feeling well. Against his wishes, mom took him to the hospital at

Carthage. They diagnosed him with congestive heart failure and edema. He was then transferred to East Texas Medical Center at Tyler, Texas. After several days a cardiologist talked to mom and dad and told them if dad's heart didn't improve, they were going to "shock" it to see if they could get it to beat in the correct rhythm again.

The next day, Leroy Hassler knocked on my dad's hospital door. Jerry Morris had told Leroy that dad was in the hospital. God immediately burdened Leroy's heart about my father. Even though my dad had not seen Mr. Hassler in over 40 years and could not see him from where he was sitting, he instantly recognized Leroy's voice. They visited a while and then Mr. Hassler asked my dad about being saved. Dad had not attended church services since he was a little boy. My mother took my sister and me to church, but my father would not go with us.

Dad admitted to Mr. Hassler that he was not saved. **Mr. Hassler led my father to Christ.** Mom and I had been taking turns staying with dad at the hospital. It was her turn so thankfully; she was there when this happened.

I came later that day and dad told me about his visit with Mr. Hassler. I can honestly say that dad was very happy that Mr. Hassler had stopped by. The doctors decided that dad's heart was not getting any better and that it needed to be shocked. The nurses were preparing dad for this when he died of a massive heart attack.

If Jerry Morris had not told Leroy Hassler that Dad was in the hospital, **if** Leroy had been in Africa, or **if** Leroy had been too busy to visit a lost friend, **if** Dad had not been in the right frame of mind to accept Christ. There are numerous "ifs," but I know why all this happened – it was God's plan.

About two months after Dad died, mom told me that the only thing that kept her from going completely crazy was the fact Dad was saved before he died. With his bad health and cancer, she had really been worrying about it.

From Texas to Alabama to Africa, Leroy Hassler is spreading the gospel to those in need. If you have a minute or two, please stop and pray for his missionary work. Thank you!

THE MIRACLE OF GOD'S TIMING
By Leroy Hassler

The above story about Mike Hartless happened a few years ago, but we never put Mike's daughter's report in print. I was home here in Gladewater but was having to get around on a walker because of a bad knee and was having knee surgery soon. I was advised not to make the 25-mile trip to Tyler, Texas and not to walk any more than necessary but God had burdened my heart for Mike's soul. Once I got to the hospital, which is very large, after walking down long halls, I found out I was in the wrong hospital and had to go to another large hospital nearby.

Despite the damaged knee and the difficulty walking, I left the walker at home and prayed that God would use me to reach Mike Hartless. I found out that many others had prayed for Mike's conversion. I thank God that Jerry Morris, a longtime friend I used to ride the school bus with, let me know of Mike's stay in the hospital. I attended Mike's funeral service and had much comfort knowing Mike was with our Lord.

Most of the people I have led to the Lord, I have led them to Christ in the first 15 minutes after I met them. God gave me the privilege of leading 5 people from age 73 to 84 to Christ during a revival meeting in Alabama in 1982. The pastor said that all of them followed through with their decision and lived for the Lord the rest of their lives. I take no credit for this but give God all the Glory!

If God can use me He can use you. Find someone and tell them about Jesus.

ZAMBIA TRIP

By Don Hayhurst

In June 2001, I had the privilege of being involved in a ten-day International Commission crusade in Zambia. It was on this trip that I met Leroy Hassler and was impacted by his life and ministry.

He and I were assigned as roommates, and each assigned to a different project. I would preach in a local church, and Leroy would be involved in an area wide crusade. Each evening we would return to our room and share what God was doing in the area we were serving and spend time together praying for a movement of God. It was during one of those evenings that we felt the presence of God in a most powerful way. I had the privilege of attending one of Leroy's evening services, when a death occurred in my assigned African church, canceling the evening services. Leroy preached a very simple gospel message and multitudes responded to the invitation to accept Christ. When the ten days were over and we were preparing to leave Zambia, I learned we needed a new $50 bill, as a bribe, to be able to leave the country. I had used all my money, except $20, to help purchase Bibles for the church I was working with. Leroy very graciously gave me the $50 so I could get on the plane.

The impact Africa, and especially Leroy, made on my life was so great, I returned to Ghana the next year to participate in another crusade. Unfortunately, I picked up a virus on the trip to Zambia and my doctors warned me to discontinue the overseas trips.

After returning to the states, Leroy and I have continued to stay in contact. I invited him to come to Bethel Baptist Church, Roswell, New Mexico to preach a revival for me. God used his messages to speak especially to my heart, as well as several people in the congregation. Over the years, my wife and I have contributed to the projects and needs he has shared with those who support his ministry.

I have known many pastors, evangelists, and Christian workers over the years, and I have never known a more humble, devoted man (and wife) to the cause of Christ. Leroy and Ann have always put the cause of Christ ahead of their desires and needs! I have not only been amazed, but also blessed and challenged by their commitment to Zambia, as they provide resources to show the Jesus film, start churches, and train indigenous pastors. I consider Leroy a friend and thank God for allowing me the joy and privilege of knowing him.

**Eugene Narth and team prepare to distribute Bibles
sent from Hassler Ministries.**

THIS PILGRIM'S PROGRESS
by Paul Stewart

In 1954, I was born in a small town in rural North Carolina named Lewisville. Most folks were farmers or related to farm families. Many worked in nearby Winston-Salem at the factories and then also farmed part-time on small

Paul Stewart and African Interpreter

family farms. I was in one of the latter families.

My parents were Charlie and Magdalene Stewart. They did a good job of raising me along with my two brothers, Michael and James. We were all in church every time the doors were open. Over the years we all heard a lot of good preaching by our pastor, Otis Clampitt.

When I was eleven years old, during a week of meetings with a guest preacher, I gave my heart to Jesus. I was under conviction of my sin and the Holy Spirit won out! I began my life with Jesus at the helm in 1965. I didn't know then where I would be going in life or what I would do, but I knew that I wanted to follow Jesus.

My first thought was that I wanted to farm like my grandfathers. Both Paul Pegram and Lindsay Stewart were tobacco farmers. I loved helping them both when I was growing up. Something about the raw earth between my toes and the joy of seeing the crops through from seed to harvest gave a great deal of satisfaction to me. Yes, I was going to be a farmer!

During all the years of hearing Preacher Clampitt's messages, he always stressed that a believer should be sowing the "good seed of the Word." He preached it; missionaries preached it; evangelists preached it; and God's Word preached it to me. Over time, I started to get it… there was a world of lost and dying people that needed the Gospel of Jesus Christ!

When I was sixteen years old, I was asked to teach a class of first and second graders in Bible School. I was given materials to study and I did study.

A few weeks after I had committed to teach Vacation Bible School, my agriculture teacher from West Forsyth High School asked me if I would go to the state competition to compete in the forestry division. I was elated! But when he told me the dates and I told him I could not go. He was disappointed. The competition was the same week of Bible School. Looking back, I know it was one of the best decisions I had made in my spiritual life. A little boy named Bobby gave his life to Jesus in Bible School. He was the first fruit of what was to become a passion in my life.

Around the time of my junior year in high school, I experienced another "passion" in my life. This passion had a name, Joy Darlene Harper! God definitely knew what He was doing when he put her in my life. We had been acquainted since we were four years old. Her mother had received Christ and started attending my home church, Immanuel Baptist, in Clemmons, North Carolina. My wife says she almost immediately laid claim to me at four years of age! I am a boy, a male, a man. I am a little slow, but at last I caught up. We have been happily married for almost forty-eight years at the time of this writing. God has blessed us with four children, their spouses, and thirteen grandchildren. God is good!

My wife and I married after high school. We both started out at public work and part-time farming. When the children started coming, we made a decision that as the Lord provided, she would stay at home with the children while I would do what I could do to provide. This was a decision we have always been glad we made. We believe God honored our putting His way of life for us as a priority. Mama at home nurturing, while Daddy is out providing, is a great biblical principle. All of our children trusted Christ early in life and have followed their decisions with good and godly choices of their own.

We were thriving in our home-life. We were thriving in our church-life. During our years as adults, we were involved in the whole life of our church. During our time of lay ministry, we saw over 150 people come to Christ through Sunday school,

VBS, and youth camp ministry. We were happy and loved the life that God had given us.

One Sunday morning, after Dr. Howard Wilburn had filled the pulpit at Immanuel Baptist, I told my wife, Joy, that I wanted to speak to her about something. The children were all busy with different Sunday afternoon activities, so we took a walk. I sort-of said to her, nervously, as we were walking, "Joy, I believe that..." and she finished the sentence, "the Lord wants you to go to Piedmont Bible College." How did she know? That is our God at work!

The next five years were: go to work, make hay, go to classes, write papers, do ministry, fix fences, feed cows, repeat, repeat, repeat. God got us through it all. I finished college at age forty-two; now what?

Prior to the last year of Piedmont Bible College, I saw an old movie that was put out by Bob Jones University. The name of it was "Sheffey." It was about an itinerant preacher of the 1800s named Robert Sheffey. He rode over parts of Virginia and Tennessee on horseback reaching people with the Gospel. In one scene, he prayed over someone saying, "Lord, before I die let me hear about this boy bringing 1,000 souls to Christ." That prayer so gripped my heart that I prayed that God would use me to do the same: 1,000 souls for Christ. How would that happen? When would it happen?

In 1995, prior to graduation from Piedmont, I resigned my positions at Immanuel Baptist Church (deacon, youth and camp director, and Sunday school teacher). Our family attended Blaise Baptist Church in Mocksville, N.C. for a short time. God had a plan. The pastor, Glen Sellers, recommended that I visit a friend who pastored Mountain View Baptist Church in Hamptonville, N.C. Pastor Tim Tucker and Mountain View was part of God's plan for teaching me more about ministry and missions. During the years there, we were able to minister to hundreds of children and youth. Pastor Tucker said he had not seen anybody as gifted in evangelism as my family. We experienced something new at Mountain View – short term missions. That was a real eye opener to me and my family. During the time at Mountain View, with youth ministry and mission trips, God used us to reach hundreds to His Son.

God called me to pastor Shady Grove Baptist in Boonville, N.C. in year 2000. This was a wonderful church with mission minded people. One of the ladies who is now in Heaven, Marie Vestal, said God was using me and my family to accomplish an answer to prayers she and her deceased husband had prayed for many years. The church was growing and new families were coming in. Ministry opportunities multiplied. We added a Youth position, hired a youth pastor, and were seeing good discipleship and growth in peoples' lives.

Short term mission opportunities multiplied. During a trip to Brazil, the prayer I had made earlier in life was realized in reality... 1,000 people had been won to Christ! That goal was reached. I said, "Now what?" to the Lord. I came to the conclusion that a new goal needed to be set: 10,000 souls!

Local ministry continued, the church continued growing, and trips were made to Jamaica, Honduras, and Brazil. In just a few short years through all aspects of ministry that number came closer and closer. Many young people and adults were reaching out and growing in the mission vision of their pastor. Sister churches were helping in the vision. One church in particular, Charity Baptist of Boonville, came alongside us and we experienced God's vision altogether. Their pastor, Eddie Driver, and I, became close friends.

An experience he had prior to my meeting him was soon to bring a change to my way of life. Eddie had been on a mission trip with an evangelist from Texas. He said that he wanted me to meet him. One day he asked if he could introduce his friend to me, Evangelist Leroy Hassler. At the time, Leroy was holding revival services at Eddie's. Brother Leroy came over to Shady Grove and we met. He wanted to see a portable sound system that I had purchased and used on a few trips with Brother Eddie. I pulled it out of storage, set it up in less than five minutes, and handed him the microphone. It blasted his voice clearly for a half mile. He said, "I need that in Zambia." The next trip to Zambia was in May of 2004. Arrangements were made to experience Zambia with Brother Leroy, Eddie Driver, and myself.

While in Zambia in 2004, several things happened. That goal of 10,000 souls were realized. A new goal of 100,000 was made. Brother Leroy Hassler taught me a new and better way for doing missions for what I believe to be my life's calling: Missions-Evangelism! The North Carolina Baptists and the Southern Baptist Convention had been encouraging people to adopt a people group or a country and invest in them for the long haul. For the next fourteen years as the pastor of Shady Grove Baptist, I was enabled to lead fourteen teams in Lusaka, Zambia. Teams of Zambian nationals were led mainly by Pastor Michael Sikaonga and me. We were usually preaching in schools by day and sharing the "Jesus Film" at night for ten to fourteen days per trip. It wasn't long before the 100,000 goal was reached, then 200,000, 300,000… The goal for one million was set in 2013. By 2018 that was surpassed. Thank you, Lord; thank you Shady Grove; thank you Leroy Hassler. Thank you, Pastor Michael Sikaonga and family for being boots on the ground in Zambia. Thank you everyone that helped over the years to challenge my heart to step out of my box and follow Him.

2018 was another time of decision. I was 64 years old. For most, it is a time to think of retiring. My wife and I agreed that we would not retire but would retread. Redirection. I resigned Shady Grove as Pastor in June of 2018. We started a ministry, PS 121 Ministries. I and my wife are involved in Springs of Life Camp in Patrick Springs, Virginia. We preach and teach young people for one week a year. We do handy man work there part-time. My wife and I serve at Triple Cross Cowboy Church part-time also. They are a wonderful church and we are honored to serve there. We do work with the NC Baptist in emergency work: feeding, collecting food, clothes, and supplies, and doing tear-outs. We speak at churches, clubs, and wherever we can to raise funds for national pastors to enable a year-round school ministry (instead of one or two weeks a year). In 2018, the gospel was preached to over 3/4 million students and teachers in Zambia. 2019 saw over 1.5 million. 2020 (Covid-19 and all) we are on track for 1.6 million, had a new church planted, the expansion of a school that was started in 2016, had 3,000 Bibles distributed along with hundreds of sanitizer kits, and preaching in 480 schools.

As anyone can see, God is doing a great work. Someone has said that the Gospel is free, and that statement is true. Christ designed that salvation would be free. All can afford salvation – absolutely free. However, it cost the Savior his death on the cross. The pipes to deliver the free water of life are costly. Many have graciously given to help in this work with their time, talents, and money. I urge any who would pray, to pray and ask God, "What should I do?" If you are to pray, then pray. If you are to give, then give. If you are to go, then go.

Working in His field, Paul Stewart, Galatians 6:9

Email: joy4me1954@gmail.com

HASSLER BROTHERS MEET IN GERMANY – 1945

On the left is my father, also named Leroy Hassler and my uncle Alvin Hassler, My father (1925-2012) was an officer and a B-26 Bomber pilot who was in the Battle of the Bulge. His brother Alvin Hassler, (1920-2000) was an Army Sgt. who was in the field in WWII and did not get to sleep in a bed for 3½ years, according to my uncle John Hassler. That many years of living in the field during a war must have been a miserable experience for Uncle Alvin not to mention the horrors of war. My father and his three brothers were military veterans who served 20 or more years in the U. S. military. They were born and raised in Pennsylvania.

My father must have known some high-ranking officer in order to borrow a bomber and fly across Germany to meet his brother. I regret that I did not ask him how he got permission to borrow an Air Force plane.

Both my father and his brother grew up in German speaking homes and both spoke German. Alvin was involved in the liberation of **Dachau Death camp** in Southern Germany near the end of WWII. As you may know Dachau was a part of the holocaust that slaughtered 6 million Jews. **Children 5 years of age and under were slaughtered!** As many as 1.5 million and reports of 2 million children were gassed to death, starved to death, or injected with Phenol in their little hearts, or hanged. Hitler hated the Ten Commandments and wanted every Jew killed. He also put to death many others besides Jews who disagreed with his policies.

What my father and uncle saw at Dachau Death camp cannot be put into words, as it was unspeakable and horrible beyond belief. Because he spoke fluent German, the Army put my uncle to work with the Jews who were alive at Dachau and helping them get on with their lives after being in the midst of such a terrible slaughter. And since my father was no longer needed as a bomber pilot, they put his German language to use by being put in charge of German prisoners of war. **THE HOLOCAUST MUST NEVER BE FOROTTEN AND MUST NEVER HAPPEN AGAIN!**

THE AMERICAN HOLOCAUST!

Fifty and probably more than sixty million babies have been slaughtered in the U. S. abortion mills. A child is a human being at the time of conception. They are not fetuses but living human beings.

You are probably thinking this is different from the Jews who were slaughtered in the holocaust. But there is no difference, none whatsoever. Murder is murder. A political

63

party that backs abortion is not going to get my vote and should not get the vote of any Christian or Jew. When you side with the murder of innocent unborn children you take part in that sin.

Murdering innocent unborn children is only a small step away from taking the lives of the elderly or anyone else who disagrees with them. In my opinion, to date, President Trump is the greatest friend a Christian or Jew ever had in my lifetime. He was a friend of Christians, Jews, and Israel.

God has not heavily judged America because many righteous people continue praying and living in the U. S. A. Also it must never be overlooked that we are on Israel's side and God highly approves of that. God blesses those who bless Israel. The mercy and grace of God is beyond our comprehension. Let us not forget that revival comes at the darkest hour and the most unexpected time. Pray for revival and mercy.

PRAYER

~

My Experiences with the Power of God in Answered Prayer

By Leroy Hassler

"Call unto me, and I will answer thee, and show thee great and mighty things, which thou knowest not." – Jeremiah 33:3

WHY I KNOW GOD ANSWERS PRAYERS

There is only one almighty, all-powerful God of all creation, and nothing can be compared to Him, absolutely nothing. If we could fully grasp and experience the power and greatness of our God, we would be truly awestruck in His presence. We would realize that we have access to someone who has the power to meet any need in the scope of His will. Prayer gives us this access and should never be our last resort, but the very first thing we do in all our needs and encounters in life. If we would but pray more, we would know more about how God answers our prayers. The following pages include a few my personal examples of God-answered prayers.

During the mid-1970s, my wife and I had the privilege to live in Dothan, Alabama. We both met God in a powerful life-changing way there, and that encounter altered, permanently,

65

the course of our lives. We were members of Cloverdale Baptist Church, which maintained a revival-like atmosphere. Some people commented that when you drove onto the parking lot, you came into the presence of God even before entering the church. If you have ever been a part of a church like that, you will never forget the experience. My wife and I experienced a great revival in our lives at Cloverdale. Many times, there, we were overpowered by the presence and power of God while living in that area of the United States.

Henry A. Johnson was the pastor of Cloverdale Baptist Church when we lived in the area. We witnessed God using him mightily. One evening, I met with a group of about twenty people in the pastor's office. We joined hands and prayed for my mother to be saved. I remember the atmosphere was super-charged with the holy and mighty presence of God at the close of that prayer time. Although I did not grow up in my mother's home (my grandparents, Judge and Mrs. H. L. Prescott, raised me), I had a great burden for my mother's salvation.

My mother was not only lost but living in an atmosphere that seemed to be working against her ever coming to know the Lord. She owned a nightclub in Houston, Texas. (I'll not mention the name of her club because I do not want to advertise the devil's business. Alcohol has destroyed more homes and relationships than anyone can possibly know.) Sometime after we had prayed for my mother, while she was tending the bar at her club, a man at the bar suddenly slammed his beer down on the bar and said, "I have got to get right with God!" He left the bar and became a committed Christian. Years later, he was on the staff of one of America's largest Baptist churches. God began getting my mother's attention through the actions of that man at her club.

About that same time, one of my mother's best friends, who was in good health, dropped dead at age fifty. God used that event to, once again, get my mother's attention. All the while, my wife and I prayed daily for her. She even came to hear me preach during that time and, according to some people who sat behind her, she got under such conviction that the left the service trembling. Not long after that, she decided to sell her night club and moved to a new city. She left her circle of friends and made new ones. She tried as best as she knew how to change her life.

One night, in 1977, my wife woke me up and said, "Your mother is on the phone and she wants to be saved." I quickly got up and talked with her.

"Son," she said. "I moved to another city, changed my friends, and started a new job, but still, I am not happy. I feel like God is after me; what do I do?" It was my joy to tell her, from the Word of God, how to be saved and led her in the sinner's prayer. God made an amazing change in her life, something that always happens when you are saved.

A few years later, I preached a revival in her town. At the end of the service, during the invitation, she made her public profession of faith in Jesus Christ and joined the church. The church asked me to baptize my mother which I gladly did. No one can tell me that God did not intervene in my mother's life in answer to the prayers of my wife and me, as well as the prayers of others who prayed. I know God is real and really does answer prayers when they are prayed from a pure heart and one that is in line with His will.

THE ANSWERED PRAYERS OF MY MOTHER

After my mother was saved, she began setting up meetings for my wife and me to visit some of her friends for whom she was praying. One of them was a 57-year-old alcoholic lady who was in a treatment facility for alcoholism. This woman was saved when we shared the Gospel with her. Afterwards, she informed her doctor that she did not need the help of the clinic anymore as she had no desire to drink again. "What happened?" the doctor asked.

"Jesus Christ saved me," she said, "and took away my desire for alcohol."

My mother sent us to another home in Dallas, Texas. This woman and her husband were former managers of a private nightclub. We shared the Gospel with them and sometime later, the lady trusted Christ as her Lord and Savior. About two years later, she died at age 61.

In the year 2000, I preached a revival meeting near the town where my mother lived. She had planned to attend the revival meetings every night but became ill and could not attend. She remained in the hospital during the entire revival meeting. She never recovered. I preached at her funeral service and we buried her next to her mother and father.

Even though my mother is now gone to be with the Lord, she is responsible for taking some others with her by way of her prayers, testimony, and concern. My wife and I have always kept a list of people for whom we are praying to be saved. We pray for them by name and believe in the power of prayer. A few months ago, someone called us to say that a person we were praying for had been saved. God really does answer prayers. Who are you praying for to be saved?

"And <u>when</u> they had prayed..." – Acts 4:31

IF WE HAD PRAYED

Have you ever thought about what God could reveal to us when we get to heaven? He could choose to show us all He would have done if we had really prayed. How little we value prayer is revealed by how little praying the average church or Christian prays. Think of all the great things God could and would do if we would really pray. Think of the multitude of souls that would be born into the Kingdom of God if we would really pray.

You and I may be, and in fact, are limited in the power to change things around us. But we serve a God who has unlimited power and abilities. Remember, He simply spoke, and the world was created out of nothing. He spoke again and the stars and planets came into existence. He is an all-powerful God who can do supernatural miracles, even today. We serve a God who is alive and able to handle any situation. It is exciting to think that this mighty God is not only willing to give us an audience, but is, in fact, waiting for us to call on Him.

God has chosen the work of prayer to get mighty things done for His glory. The early church prayed, and prison doors swung open so Peter could walk out. That same God is still available to the Christian today who will commit to praying. When we have such a mighty God, how can we keep from talking to Him? The great revivals of history have all been started because someone began the work of prayer and asked God for revival. Many great missionary movements have begun because of someone's prayers, somewhere on the face of the earth.

It is sometimes frustrating to try and call a close friend, when you really need to talk, and find that his phoneline is busy. But we have a great God that can answer all the calls of all His children, from all over the world. And even today, He is sitting by the prayer-line phone, waiting for a call now. When we have a God like that, why do we not talk to Him in prayer? The Bible says that He knows what we need before we ask. The problem is that we often just do not ask.

ASK!

Despite many, many great promises in the Word of God, we still do not ask. Elijah called on God in prayer, in 1 Kings 18:24, and God sent a revival to the nation of Israel and performed many mighty works on top of Mount Carmel. We read, in James 5:17, that Elijah was a man of "like passions as we are." That means he was not some super saint, but a normal person, as we are today. But he called on a supernatural God who can do supernatural things according to His will. And He did them.

The God of Elijah is our God if we have been truly converted. Furthermore, God has not changed. He is still the same supernatural God that worked miracles on Mount Carmel for Elijah, and He is waiting for us to call upon Him. I ask, again, why will we not ask God in believing prayer? It would be a sad day, instead of a glad day if, when we get to heaven, God chooses to show us all the family members, friends, and neighbors that He would have saved if we had just performed the work of prayer and asked Him for their salvation. He might

70

show us the long overdue and much-needed revival that He wanted to send to America if we had seriously prayed and trusted Him for it.

What if God reveals all He would have done in the church, if we had fervently asked Him to move in our midst in supernatural power? God desires for us to pray because prayer shows that we are depending on Him as a little child depends on his father. Whatever it is that you have need of today, if it is in His will, God is waiting for you to ask Him for it so that He can be glorified by giving you an answer—an answer by which you can praise and glorify an all-mighty, all-powerful, Holy God.

TOO BUSY TO PRAY?

If we are too busy to pray, we need to rearrange our schedules. In fact, if we are too busy to pray, we are too busy for God because He wants to fellowship with us. One of the ways He does this is through prayer. Years ago, I heard someone say, "Beware of the busy life." In all our hectic schedules, it is sad to say that one of the first things that we trim out of our schedule is time for God through prayer and the study of His Word. It is no wonder that sometimes our lives, as Christians, and our churches become so barren spiritually. The barrenness is evidence that we need to return to God and prayer.

In my life, I have found that I have time to do what I really want to do. If a man likes to fish, he takes time to fish. If he likes to spend an hour reading the paper and watching the news on television, he does so. If a lady likes to shop, almost nothing can keep her from shopping. Now these things, in themselves, are not bad, but they do reveal that we take time to do what we really want to do.

I want to encourage you to take time to pray. I have found that the morning is the best time for me to pray and read the Bible. That is not the only praying that I do, but the first part of our day is usually the best part to give to God. We cannot claim we are putting God first in our lives if we do not even try to spend time in prayer and in His Word daily. If Jesus is Lord of our lives, we will find time to do the basic things that make a successful Christian life, things like prayer and reading His love letter, the Word of God.

If you are not already doing so, the time to start doing this is now. Start today and you will not be sorry. You are not waiting for God; He is waiting for you. Spending time in real prayer is never wasted time.

PRAYING FOR A VEHICULAR TIRE JACK

In May of 1996, in Ghana, West Africa, I was doing a series of evangelistic meetings when our van broke down on a long and isolated stretch of road, out in the middle of nowhere. It was a flat tire. My interpreter, Eugene Narth, a godly African minister, informed me that our vehicle's jack was broken. Since it was late at night, traffic was at a minimum and no one would stop to help us. We had traveled many miles from our last meeting and were traveling back to the hotel in another city.

Eugene tried everything he knew to get the jack to work, but to no avail. Finally, he walked off toward a small village nearby to get help while I remained alone with the van. Sometime later, Eugene returned with no help and no jack. No one in the village had a vehicle so there was no jack to be found. We decided to pray over the jack. Afterwards, Eugene crawled underneath the van to try the jack again. It worked! Soon the tire was replaced and we were on our way again. We gave all glory and praise to God who can even heal a broken jack. We have a mighty God who is concerned about everything. Had we not prayed over that jack, we might have stayed there all night waiting for help.

ALLOWING GOD TO SHAKE US

"The place was shaken," – Acts 4:31

When people get serious and really pray, they can expect a shaking to take place. Real prayer always brings real answers and brings us in touch with a Holy God. The closer we get to Him, the more God will put the focus of His penetrating Spirit on our hearts. When He does this, you can be sure that the spiritual condition of the praying person will be revealed.

There are two responses to the convicting power of the Holy Spirit. We can refuse to obey and continue living apart from God's power or we can repent and turn to Him for useful service. When someone comes to God, there will be an inner desire to pray and be in touch with Him. You never have to beg someone to pray when they are right with God.

If your church still has a prayer meeting or if a prayer meeting is planned for a revival or other special service, why do so few attend? We know it is no problem to get a big crowd to attend a concert of a popular Christian singer, but why do so many avoid a prayer meeting like it's a plague? I believe the reason is that if we really pray, we must get completely right with God to get our prayers heard. Psalm 66:18 says, "If I regard iniquity in my heart, the Lord will not hear me." This means that if we, as Christians, hang on to sin and refuse to release sinful practices in our lives, God will not answer our prayers. He cannot work through a person who is not totally surrendered to Him. If you are not a Christian, God is not obligated to answer any of your prayers, because you are not His child.

As Christians, the more we seek to stay clean and free from known sin in our lives, the more effectively we will live the Christian life. God expects His children to be completely surrendered before Him. He desires first place in the heart of every Christian, and that means letting Jesus be Lord of our lives. It is not an option. If we are to pray effectively, Jesus must be Lord over every part of our lives.

Repentance of personal sin and complete surrender to the Lordship of Christ are necessary if we expect God to hear and answer our prayers. Many people avoid effective praying because they refuse to repent and because of this one thing, they remain out of fellowship with God. We can go through the motions of prayer, witnessing, or whatever we are doing in the Christian life, yet still miss the mark of effective praying. But believe me when I say that God wants total surrender out of you and out of me.

Many Christians view repentance as a grueling, repulsive task. It is not. Repentance should be viewed as a delight and a blessing because it will put us in fellowship with the living God of all creation. Yes, it can be difficult at times, but the difficulty lies within us. You see, sometimes it is difficult for us to turn loose of sin or habits that may be in our lives. Unrepentant sin displeases God, but it pleases Him when we repent and confess sin. And when we do, He blesses us for obeying Him in every area of our lives.

Things like pride, envy, gossip, jealousy, and many other things can and will keep God from hearing and answering our prayers. So, we will benefit greatly if we allow God to shake everything out of our lives that prevents us from having fellowship with Him. When I say fellowship, I refer to our daily walk with God. We can be saved and yet not be in fellowship with God. And when we are not in fellowship with Him, God cannot use and bless our lives as He desires.

Years ago, a friend of mine, the late Manley Beasley, was preaching a revival meeting in Alabama. A lady came up to him and asked why that for many years God had not answered her prayers concerning her lost husband being saved. Brother Manley told the lady that the problem might be within her own life. This caused her to do a lot of heart searching. When she poured her heart out before God, He began to shake things out of certain areas of her life.

One area was in dipping snuff. God told her to quit. She set her heart on obeying God and took all her cartons of snuff back to the store where she had purchased them. When the store clerk asked why, she said, "The Holy Spirit told me to bring it back and get a refund."

He looked at her. "Who told you to bring it back?"

"The Lord told me to bring it back and get a refund."

Tears began running down the clerk's face. "Lady, can you please tell me how to get saved?" That lady led the store clerk to Christ because she obeyed her Lord.

There is not a command in the Bible to quit dipping snuff. There are, however, principles dealing with a Christian's body being the temple of the Holy Spirit and we know that snuff can be harmful to the body. The point is that if God reveals something to you that is in your life that does not please Him, you need to do whatever is necessary to make it right. If you have offended someone, you need to go to them and ask them to forgive you. Bitterness and a lack of forgiveness will keep our prayers from getting answered.

In the lives of most Christians, it is little things that they already know are wrong that keep God from using and blessing them. These little areas of non-surrender also keep the power of the Holy Spirit from working in our lives. Without His power, we cannot pray effectively or do anything else properly pertaining to the Kingdom of God. The prophet Samuel told King Saul that the Lord God had anointed Saul to be king and to now go and "utterly destroy" the pagan city of Amalek, "all that they have and spare them not" (1 Samuel 15:3). Saul went and did as instructed, except that he did not destroy the king of the Amalekites and he saved the choice stock of the sheep, oxen, other choice animals, "and all that was good" (v. 9). When confronted by Samuel, Saul said that he saved the best to give as a sacrifice to God. "And Samuel said, 'Hath the Lord as great delight in burnt offerings and sacrifices, as in obeying the voice

Leroy preaching at Central Baptist Church, Carthage, Texas – 1975

of the Lord? Behold, to obey is better than sacrifice, and to hearken than the fat of rams.'" (v. 22). The point made is that you cannot please God in disobedience and your prayers will not be answered.

We must allow God to put us in a position to pray effectively. This involves cooperation with the leading of the Spirit of God. This is where we often fail in prayer. God is more interested in you being in fellowship with Him than you are in being in fellowship with Him. If you really desire to be totally surrendered before God, He will do all that is needed to reveal the things which keep that from happening; but then we must repent and obey God. That old Christian hymn, "Trust and Obey," is a good motto by which to live the Christian life. There is no other way to do it right.

Effective prayer is more than just uttering words; it is more than just saying everything correctly. Effective prayer must come out of a heart that is surrendered to the Living God. The Holy Spirit is the one who gives direction, life, and energy to our prayers. He is the one Who shows what to pray for and how to pray. That is why we must surrender daily to the Lordship of Christ, so that the Holy Spirit can lead and work through our lives.

Now, are you willing to allow God to shake you and control your life?

The oldest church Leroy Hassler has ever preached in. This was during the late 1990's on the South Western coast of South India. The church was built in 1503 and it is the oldest European church in India. Famous explorer Vasco da Gama was buried in the church floor in 1524. The church is at Cochin.

PRAYER AND EVANGELISM

Like effective prayers, effective evangelism always begins with a burdened heart that calls out to the Living God in prayer. Evangelism that is not bathed in prayer will always be weak and ineffective. Years ago, many Christians had prayer lists that contained the names of specific lost people that they were asking God to save. I am sure some people still have lists like that, but, sadly, most Christians are not praying regularly for specific lost people to be saved.

When I first starting preaching revival meetings in 1974, usually, at the end of an evangelistic service, church members would come to me and say, "Pray for my father, he is lost." Some would ask prayer for friends at school who are lost or friends at work who are lost. Sadly, most of the prayer requests that I get now are for material things. This reveals how far we have drifted away from God in a few short years.

More than anything else in the world, God is interested in lost people being saved and brought into the Kingdom. As far as I know, after studying the Bible since 1973, before someone is saved, you can be sure that God will use someone to pray for that person to be saved. Prayer is the first step in reaching the lost for Christ.

There is more that you can do, besides prayer, to reach the lost, but without prayer, we have made a faulty start. During 1980 or 1981, I was preaching a revival meeting in the state of Alabama. After one of the evening services, the pastor and I were at the church for about an hour just visiting with each other. A man, about fifty years of age, came back to the church. He was in tears. He had just been over to his parent's house and attempted to witnessed to them. Afterwards, they asked him to leave and to never come back again to talk with them about Christ. We prayed with and for the man and his parents. The pastor said that we would go over to his parent's house the next day and witness to them.

When we got to their house, their grandson, who was well over six feet tall, saw us from the barn. He immediately fell to his knees and with tears running down his cheeks, started praying, "O God, save my grandparents." When we got to the front door, I asked the two people if I could speak to them for about five minutes. To my surprise, they answered, "Yes." I shared the plan of salvation with them and when I finished, asked if they would like to pray and ask Christ to save them. The man, eighty years old and an alcoholic, immediately got on his knees by the couch and prayed for Christ to save him. Next, the lady, eighty-four years old, said that she wanted to be saved and prayed to receive Christ.

After this, the pastor and I returned to his home. He received a message from another lady, seventy-three years old. She had just talked with the lady that we had led to Christ earlier. This lady also wanted to be saved. The pastor told me later that all these people followed through with their decisions and were faithful to the Lord until He called them home.

These testimonies are not to say that I am a great witness but is a testimony to our powerful God who hears and answers prayer. He will use anyone who will get right with Him and obey Him. If you do not have a prayer list of persons that you are asking God to save, I want to challenge you to start one today. Ask God who He wants you to put on your list and start lifting their names before the heavenly Father.

God blesses and honors genuine prayers—prayers from your heart. He will bless you if you remain faithful in prayer. There is nothing that is or no one who is too hard for our powerful God to change or save. His call to the prophet Jeremiah is still valid today: "Call unto me, and I will answer thee and show thee great and mighty things, which thou knowest not." (Jeremiah 33:3) We can trust what God has said.

SIX CARS AND TWO VANS! GOD ANSWERS OUR PRAYERS

"And [Jesus] did not do many mighty works there because of their unbelief." – Matthew 13:58

You would think that among born again, truly converted people, there would not be any skeptics, yet that is not the case. In the early 1990s, my wife and I were praying for a car. After many prayers, we were confident that God would provide one. We had reached this position by faith and began believing that the answer was on the way.

Sometime after that, an evangelist friend, Bill Blankenship of White Oak, Texas, (who is now with the Lord) called and said that God had impressed him to give us their car. He was a godly, praying man who made a lasting impression on us. The car was a used Pontiac Bonneville, but still in extremely good shape. We preferred and needed a used car because there would be no monthly payments. This was indeed a gift from God through a godly person.

Not long after receiving the car, we drove onto the parking lot of a large church and saw a man we knew. We told him how God had provided us with the car and how happy we were with it. Many others, besides us, were praying for our car need and we were rejoicing how God had answered the prayers of many.

I thought the man, a church leader, would rejoice with us. Instead, he looked at us coldly and asked, "What are you going to do when that one breaks down?"

"Sir, God will provide another one," I answered calmly. Since then, our Lord has provided us a total of eight vehicles.

God almost never answers the prayers of skeptical and unbelieving Christians. Unbelief, like any other sin, will kill your prayer life and break your fellowship with the Living God. If that man could not believe God had given us this car, how could he believe that God could provide eight? Do not allow unbelief to separate you from your fellowship with God.

BELIEF AND PATIENCE IN PRAYER

When you are praying for something, you may have to be very patient because God answers in His own time and in His own way. Impatient people rarely see answers to prayer. During the 1980s, a friend of ours taught prayer seminars all over the state of Texas. During the seminar, he asked church members, "Have you ever received a direct answer to your prayer?" More than fifty percent said, "No."

This is an astounding response. God moves His church and His work forward by means of prayer. The sad fact is that many say words that reach no higher than the ceiling of a building, but few pray prayers that reach God, Himself.

One of the great things about doing ministry around the world is the wonderful Christians that you meet and get to really know. One of the most impressive, spiritual men I know is a missionary in Africa that I have personally met and have worked with on several mission trips. He receives no salary from a denomination but lives a life of faith. He moved his family to Africa and lives in the African bush country with little or nothing. This is his ministry, and he walks throughout the bush country with no vehicle.

One time, he said he got lost and walked for four days before finding his way back to his home. This is the African bush country where lions and leopards stalk their prey. Yet, because of his faith, he said he walked with great joy until he found his way out. Since then, God has provided him with several four-wheel-drive vehicles, which helps him through the muddy, rainy seasons and the always rough terrain of the African bush country.

This missionary has discovered that living by faith is one of life's greatest blessings. Some of the most spiritual people my wife and I have met are the ones who live by faith. Genuine faith often does not come until we are forced into the presence of God by a great need or pressing circumstances.

Jesus said, "What things soever you desire, when you pray, believe that you receive them, and you shall have them." (Mark 11:24) Genuine, effective prayers always move beyond asking into believing. Sin keeps most folks from real prayer and real faith. Sin always takes the Christian away from God and certainly away from real praying.

THE HARLEY-DAVIDSON OR WHEN GOD SAID YES, THEN NO

Years ago, I was bitten by the Harley-Davidson motorcycle bug. Like many adults my age, I had wanted a motorcycle ever since I was in the fifth or sixth grade. My grandfather, H. L. "Lee" Prescott, and his wife, Maudie, who raised me, never allowed me to have a motorcycle. Although paying for it was never an issue, since I worked all my life, I listened to and obeyed my incredibly wise grandfather. It was the right thing to do and I respected him very much. His influence continues to guide my life in many ways to this very day.

My grandparents have long since gone to be with the Lord. So, when the motorcycle bug bit me, I began asking God for permission to buy a certain Harley-Davidson. Since I had witnessed God answer my prayers many times, I knew there was nothing too great for Him to do. After praying for some time, I felt that it was God's will for me to have a Harley-Davidson. However, during that level of faith, God impressed me not to ever have a motorcycle. I simply said, "God, if You do not want me to have one, that settles it. I do not want one."

My life continued without the desire for a motorcycle. I learned that when God says "No," it's as good as Him saying "Yes" or "Wait." I remember praying for something else I thought I really needed. But during prayer, God said, "No." I laughed out loud and said in my heart, "Okay God, if You do not want me to have it, I am happy without it." I knew God's "No" answer was His best answer for me.

Later on, my wife and I were at church one Sunday. A deacon came to me and said, "I have a Harley-Davidson motorcycle that I want to give you." When he described it, it was exactly the one I had been praying for right down to the model and engine size. But I refused the offer and wouldn't even go down to look at it. He wanted me to come see it and ride it. I said, "No."

"Well," he said, "Is it okay if I sell it and donate the money to your overseas ministry?"

"That would be fine," I said. "Thank you very much." A few Sundays later, that deacon walked over to me and handed me a check made out to Hassler Evangelistic Ministries. We thanked him and our Lord for providing for our needs.

Looking back, if I had taken the motorcycle and had a wreck, I might have been killed or severely injured to the extent that I would not have completed the mission God had called me to do, and that is to reach the millions of souls our ministry has reached for Christ. My wife and I make it our aim not to allow anything or any involvement to keep us from completing the goal of our mission and ministry.

Sometimes what we want and ask God for might not be the best thing for us. Years ago, a godly young musician wanted an airplane by which to travel to his concerts. Although he was a great man of God and loved by many, some of his friends warned him about owning a plane. He got one anyway and one day, while taking off, the plane crashed and killed everyone on board, including two of his children. Only God knows why this happened and what this man and his children could have become had not this tragic death occurred. This is simply a reminder that we must be careful what we ask God for and if it is His will.

Getting a clear answer from God takes time. Many Christians in an affluent society want everything in a hurry. We have a thriving economy built on getting things in a hurry. But you must not treat our Lord that way. He must be treated with respect and patience. God is never in a hurry yet is always on time with His answers.

You may get your answer through reading the Bible. God may speak to you through a passage of Scripture and, in your heart, you will know that He is speaking to you. If this has never happened to you, I can hardly describe the feeling of joy and peace this produces.

God may use others to give you an answer. As I was considering the motorcycle that I anticipated in answer to prayer, many people shared with me tragic stories of people who lost their lives in motorcycle wrecks. Not one of these people knew I was considering getting a motorcycle. Finally, a pastor friend of mine, who had a deep walk with the Lord, told me one of his friends died while just test-driving a motorcycle around a block. I considered that to be my final answer from God. After that, if someone had brought twenty Harley-Davidson motorcycles over to my house and said, "They are yours," I would not have taken them, except to sell for missions.

As you obey God, He gives you a clearer understanding of His ways. Without praying and waiting upon the Lord, it is impossible to grow and become a person of faith—a person who can discern the will of God. We must walk and live in the light of His presence. Many stumble at this point. If we do not obey God, He will not hear, much less answer, our prayers. Obedience is not optional if you want to have an effective prayer life. This obedience starts with little things, the routine things and events of your every-day life.

A friend of mine said that he went $50,000 in debt because he did not obey God in a matter of much less than ten dollars. Obedience (or rebellion) starts with little things and will always lead to bigger things. Now is the time to start obeying God in every detail of your life. If you can be happy living in disobedience, you possibly have never been saved. Saved people cannot be happy living a life that is out of harmony with God's will.

I do not want to leave you with the impression that it is wrong to have a motorcycle, a car, or a rocket ship, for that matter. The point is that the will of God should be considered in what we have or what we do not have. We are told in the Word of God to pray about everything, and in asking God, we at times, will have to be content with a "no" answer. Many times, the no is for our own good and certainly for His glory.

REVIVAL

~

Leroy and an interpreter preparing to preach to students in India.

GOD STILL HAS THE POWER

"I am the Lord, I change not..." – Malachi 3:6a

Malachi 3:6 is one of the most encouraging verses in all the Bible to me. It is encouraging because it reveals some of the nature and character of God. God is unchanging. Our friends can and do sometimes change. Our environment is changing. Our job can change and may not exist tomorrow. The economy is everchanging. But God never changes. He is constant and consistent.

87

If God never changes, that means what He has done in the past, He can still do today. God has the power to do whatever is in the scope of His will. To those who want it, God's will is not limited and His purposes can be fulfilled in the lives of those who are yielded to Him.

Our awesome God has the power to save the most hardened person in the town or area that you live in. No one can resist His power. Whatever God did in the past, if it is His will, He can do today without fail. Your lights may go off in your home, but there is never a power shortage with our God.

Many years ago, I had a pastor friend who told me the story of his conversion. He said, "I was in a bar, completely drunk, and giving no thought to God. A few minutes later, it seemed that the power and presence of God came into that bar. It was then that I asked the Lord to save me. God saved me and sobered me up. Later on, he called me to preach. I know what and why it happened that day. My conversion was an answer to my mother's prayers."

We do not need another day of Pentecost, as described in Acts, Chapter 2. But we certainly need the power that was released on that day. In Acts 4:31, the church was in need of a fresh outpouring of the power of God, so the believers gathered and prayed until the place where they were praying was literally shaken by the power of God. If you do not believe that can happen today, you are sadly mistaken. Duncan Campbell experienced the same shaking in a prayer meeting on Lewis Island, off the cost of Scotland. We still have the same God, even though Duncan Campbell has gone on to heaven. But that one and the same God still has the same power to send revival as He did on the island where Campbell was preaching the Word of God.

If you are not experiencing the power of God (meaning, the fullness of the Holy Spirit) in your own life, you can be assured that the fault is not a power shortage on God's part. God has the power, in fact, all power is in His hands and control, and He will send it to a willing person or church who is clean and committed to obeying Him. God's power is not for the disobedient, nor is it for the person who is unwilling to make a clean break with known sin in their heart.

When talking about revival, we are speaking about a supernatural release of God's power and presence. Revival is getting into the presence of God and allowing Him to fill us to the fullest extent of our need on His behalf.

If God seems far away, the problem usually lies within us. God saved us to have fellowship with us and He is more than willing to be real to us, if we are willing to be all that He wants us to be. The God of Elijah and the God of John the Baptist is still available to those who earnestly seek Him with all of their hearts today. He still has, in His grasp, the same unlimited power to change whatever and whoever needs His changing touch.

Sometimes we need to be reminded of the power of prayer. We are praying to the God of this universe; He is all-powerful and unchanging. Many pray as if they're praying to someone who may not have the power to answer their prayers. But if you are a Christian, you should believe without a doubt that God is powerful enough to bring a God-sent revival for souls to be saved, for nations to be evangelized, and for the devil to be shaken and terrified. The devil is terrified when God's people really pray. That is why he will do all he can to stop them from praying.

You need to <u>pray for revival</u>. Do not let anything stop you from praying for revival. God has all the power needed to revive an individual, church, or country. We are on the winning side because of what our Lord did at Calvary. As the song says, the blood Jesus shed will never lose its power. We have guaranteed access to God because of the blood sacrifice of our Savior. So <u>pray, and pray some more for God-sent revival</u>. This is what we need and nothing less.

REVIVAL ~ GOD DEMANDS WE PAY THE PRICE

"Even from the days of your fathers, ye are gone away from mine ordinances and have not kept them. Return unto me, and I will return unto you, saith the Lord of host." – Malachi 3:7

In Malachi's day, God's people had drifted away from obeying Him from their hearts and we're only going through the motions of serving Him. But revival must always start with the people of God. It is not the White House that is in the greatest need of revival, but God's House, the Church. In Acts 2, the church began in supernatural power, but by Acts 4, they were in need of a fresh outpouring of the power of God. Revival involves a return to a total commitment to the Lordship of Jesus Christ. Lost people do not need revival; they need to be saved. It is the people of God, church members, who have been born again and bought with the precious blood of the Lamb of God. It is the people of God who drift away from Him and in need of revival.

Revival usually starts with one person or a few people in the church who see their powerlessness, their sin, their rebellion, and how far they are from New Testament Christianity. They must see this and must return to the living God, who is the only One who can change them into what He, alone, intended them to be. It is then that revival will spread through the church. God always works with the committed few who are seeking Him with all their hearts. We must be willing to be the committed few. Someone has said if you can go on living without revival, then you will probably go on without revival. We must seriously seek the Lord.

THE PRICE OF REVIVAL SPELLED OUT

Malachi 3:7 says, "Return unto Me!" Revival is always a return to God on the part of God's people. The price is repentance; it is absolutely necessary that God's people repent of sin in their lives in order to return all the way back to God. We, as Christians, must see how far we have drifted from New Testament Christianity for revival to come to us. Repentance is a change of mind, leading to a change of heart, that will result in a change of actions or lifestyle. Just being sorry about your sin and your failures to obey God is not repentance.

NO PERSON IS EVER SAVED WITHOUT FAITH AND REPENTANCE

Faith and repentance are twin graces that go hand in hand in salvation. The Christian lifestyle is a life of repentance and faith. Any time you allow known sin to get into your life, as a Christian, you break fellowship with God and, in fact, distance yourself from God. That also brings about a loss of the peace, power, and presence of God. It is sad, but true, that most

Christians today hardly know what it means to have the peace, power, and manifest presence of God in their lives.

An effective Christian life is one of constant repentance, or turning away from sin, the world, and living a life dominated by self and selfish desires. The normal Christian life, as portrayed in the Bible, is one of total abandonment to God. If you can be happy with less than that, you may well have never genuinely been saved. Saved people cannot be happy while out from under God's control and the Lordship of Christ.

In the late 1970s, while I was preaching, a couple became upset over my message, stood up, and walked out. They stopped in the church parking lot. One of them said, "What Brother Hassler said is right. We need to be saved." They came back inside and responded to the invitation, giving their lives to Christ. The last I heard of them, they were still serving the Lord.

In 1979, in another revival meeting, a couple, seated up front, got up and left while I was preaching. It is not uncommon for people to get upset and leave when a preacher is preaching the uncompromising Word of God, which is the way I preach. While I was preaching, I thought about their leaving. (I can assure you that a man can preach and think at the same time.) When God brings conviction into your heart, you may try and do anything but repent.

Later, before the service ended, that same couple returned, carrying a large paper sack. When the invitation was given, they came forward, with the sack, and got right with God. One of them said, "We left because we needed to get right with God, but there were some things in our house we needed to get rid of that was hurting our family and our testimony for Christ."

"Yes," the other one said. "And we had to do it now." In the sack was all kinds of beer and liquor. They truly repented. "We do not want this in our home anymore. We do not want to live our lives in a way that dishonors God."

Repentance will do just that. They made a clean break with their sinful habits. When God moves on your heart, you must repent. Nothing less is acceptable to Him.

The pastor, Herschel Sizemore at Seale Road Baptist Church, said, "After the revival service, that first Sunday morning, the carpet at the front of our church was wet in places from the tears of repentance that were shed by so many people who came and knelt at the altar seeking God and repenting of sin."

What was scheduled as a one-week revival, became two weeks instead. God came into that church and moved in mighty power. Someone had to pay the price, and many did during that two-week period. Some of the leaders in the church made public apologies to the church for their behavior.

Many, today, resist revival because it means change; yet many are unwilling to change. Most people, and many churches, fight change. Repentance will always mean a change in the direction of a person's life. Repentance is the only thing that can bring a Christian closer to God. God can do more in five minutes of real repentance than the next five years' worth of seminars that you may attend.

A pastor called me some time ago and asked, "Why is it that we can train and train people to be witnesses and soulwinners for Christ, and yet still end up with so few people who can actually win someone to Christ?"

I responded, "When a person gets totally right with God, you cannot stop them from winning people to Christ, whether they're trained or not." Do not misunderstand, a trained person will be more effective, but a person who is sold out to Jesus will be easier to train and will possess an inner drive to win souls.

MAY I ASK YOU A FEW QUESTIONS?

Let me get personal. Where do you stand in your walk with our Lord? Is He real to you or are you living a great distance from God, even as a Christian? What is your honest answer?

God did not save you to occupy a seat in a church until the end of your life. He wants your life to count for Him here and now. I do not care if you are twelve years old or eighty-five years old, it is never too late to come back to God in repentance.

Our nation needs revival. I believe God is wanting to send revival to this nation and He may be wanting to start with you. If you are saved, I can promise you that He wants you to give your life totally to Him as a Christian. If you do not feel that way, or if you are unwilling to do that, you may have never been truly saved. Saved people long to live for God and live all out for Him. Do you have that holy longing in your heart? Do you want to be all that He wants you to be?

YOU ARE SPECIAL TO GOD

If you are a Christian, you are special to God. You are so special that He sent His Son to die on a cross just for you. If you had been the only needy sinner in the world, He would have sent Christ just to die for you and your sins.

In Romans 12:1, we are told to give our lives as a living sacrifice to God. He is speaking to Christians here and is saying, in effect, "Now that you are saved, I want all of you. I want all of your time, all of your talent, and all that you are. I want everything totally signed over to Me!"

94

We have come to the place that we think submitting to the Lordship of Christ is optional or just for a few. The Lordship of Christ is for every Christian, no exceptions. This is the minimum standard for following Jesus. In Luke 14:27, Jesus said, "Whosoever doth not bear his cross, and come after me, cannot be my disciple."

The cross is a place to die on. As Christians, we must die to sin, self, the world, and the devil. Paul said, in Galatians 2:20, "I am crucified with Christ." As a Christian, God will move you to the place of making a total sellout of yourself to Him. You must sign over to Him the title deed of your life and your future.

You may be saying to yourself, "If I did that, there is no telling what God might want me to do!" This is correct. Now you are getting the picture. The sold-out life is an exciting life because the God of this universe is calling the shots and giving the orders for each and every day. Your flesh may rebel at this thought, but deep in your heart, you know I am right. Personal revival starts with personal repentance and commitment to the absolute Lordship of Jesus Christ. I want to challenge you to ask God to make you willing to totally sell out to Him. If you are willing, stop reading now and seek the Lord in prayer and commitment. He is waiting to hear from you right now, so do not delay.

Any known sin in your life will hinder you from walking with Him and having His manifest presence and power on your life. You must repent of and forsake all known sin, then submit to the Lordship of Christ and seek the power of the Holy Spirit.

This might be your prayer: "God, I do not want to continue my life being less than You want me to be. I truly want to know Your power and presence in my life. I want to be obedient to You in every area of my life. I am tired of playing games with

You. I repent and ask You to change me and make me a vessel of revival."

Do not pray the above prayer if you do not mean it.

REVIVAL AND THE PROMISE FOR OBTAINING IT

"I will return unto you, saith the Lord." – Malachi 3:7

If the above part of Malachi 3:7 does not encourage you to seek the Living God, you need to ask God to wake you up. The God of this universe promised that if we would repent and return unto Him, He would return unto us. That promise is better than money in the bank. In fact, the whole Word of God is like $10 million dollars of gold buried ten feet down in your back yard. It is there and just waiting to be found. The condition of finding the gold is digging down to where it is.

The promises in the Bible all have conditions to be met. In Malachi 3:7 we must repent before God will return to us and bless us with His presence and power. Revival is locked up in the sovereignty of God, but it is amazing how a Sovereign God responds to real repentance on the part of one of His children or an entire church. The Bible says that even the angels of God rejoice over one single person who repents (Luke 15:7, 10). God takes notice of repentance because that puts a person in a position to get their prayers answered and to claim the promises of God.

I would think it would be a great honor to meet with the President of the United States, but the fact is that God is waiting for us to get in such a state of repentance that He can be more real to us than any other person in the world. He can be more real than the clothes on your body or the air that you breathe. Our God is a real being that loves to reveal Himself.

In 1973 at work one day, I went to a room by myself during our lunch break and read my Bible. Shortly after reading my Bible, I began praying. It seemed like the heavens opened and I was on my face in tears at the feet of Jesus. I felt that if I had opened my eyes, I would have seen the Lord Jesus. That day, a radical change occurred in my life, causing me to repent. I saw myself as God saw me and I did not like what I saw. God was not pleased with me, so I returned to Him as a Christian. He kept His Word and returned to me, and in those few moments I gave Him my life completely. Almost immediately, I became concerned for my friends and lost people everywhere. I wept my way back to God, in repentance, and have never regretted it.

Based on my experiences and the testimony of many Godly friends, there is no other way to the reality of God's presence in our lives, as Christians. A lifestyle of repentance is essential. Sin is the enemy of God's presence being real in our lives. You cannot fellowship with God and have known sin in your life at the same time. You must repent of sin to maintain fellowship with God. There is a price to pay before you can have the promise of God's return to your life. And that price is called repentance.

As a Christian, can you think of any place you'd rather be than in the presence of God and in the center of His will? I cannot, and I think that is true of all genuine Christians. One way that you can know, with certainty, that you are saved is an awareness of God's presence and knowing that He will never leave you alone until He has all of you in complete submission to Him and His will. God is committed to His own children and just like any good parent, He wants the best for them.

It breaks the hearts of many pastors and even the heart of God, that so many Christians are seemingly content living in a state that is not all God wants them to be. The devil is happy when Christians live in a manner that is inconsistent with the Word of God. A half-hearted commitment is not a commitment that is pleasing to God. In the Book of First Samuel, King Saul tried to live like that and God removed his kingdom and gave it to David. Eventually, Saul committed suicide. Any time you try to live in a state of partial commitment to our Lord, you commit spiritual suicide and forfeit the blessing and presence of God from your life.

We must not be content living out from under the Lordship of Christ and living in a state of partial surrender, which is totally displeasing to God. My wife and I have had the unpleasant experience of preparing for company to come, getting all that was needed to treat them well, and then told, "We cannot make it; we have had a change in plans." We were disappointed and, in one instance, downright broken hearted.

It breaks the heart of God when his children do not live in submission to Him and experience His return to their lives in power. God is waiting on us; we are not waiting on Him. His heart is broken when our lives are in such a state that He cannot be real and close to us.

Some of you know the heartbreak that one has when a loved one is in the hospital and so sick that they are in an induced coma. You can be near them and yet so very far away. You want to communicate with them, but you cannot. You want to have their fellowship, but try as you may, you cannot. The sick person is not in a state to be conscious of your presence, much less enjoy your fellowship.

I feel that God is knocking on the doors of many churches and the doors of many Christians and saying, "I want your fellowship more than you could ever know. Please, please let Me in the door." Jesus Christ died on the cross, not only to save us and take us to heaven someday, but to be real to us here and now.

In Revelation 3:20, Jesus says, "Behold I stand at the door and knock: if any man hear my voice and open the door, I will come in to him, and will sup (be real) with him, and he with Me." Many use this as an evangelistic text when inviting people to trust Jesus as Lord and Savior, in personal witnessing. I have done so myself, and that is fine. But the direct and real meaning of this verse is that Jesus Christ is knocking on the door of the church, the true blood-bought believers, and wants to get inside so He can be real to them and empower them to take this generation for Christ. Christian, is He not knocking on your hearts door now and wanting to be your everything—the Alpha and Omega, in your life? He will not until you let Him in. You open the door by genuine deep repentance. He will not be real to an unrepentant Christian. He will not answer the prayers of an unrepentant Christian.

Those of you who know me, know I have made more than forty trips overseas to conduct crusades. By the grace of God, I have now preached more than 1200 messages overseas in some 19 countries. I do not mind telling you that my wife and I have had some gut-wrenching "goodbyes." It is never easy being away from the one I love more than life itself. No one said that obeying God would be easy or pleasant to your fleshly self, and it is not.

At times, the minute I walked away from my wife to go to the plane, I have had tears streaming down my face. Once on the plane, even though overseas plane tickets can cost more than $2,000.00, and I know that I was in God's will, I have come close to getting off the plane and not walking, but running, back to my lovely wife's arms. But you see, I could not do that. As I know, and she knows, I would be disobeying God. God has called me into a traveling ministry, and it is not as easy or as glamorous as it may appear on the surface.

When I leave home for an extended period, I can hardly wait for the return home. When the plane touches down, I am looking out the window for the best-looking woman in the world to me, my wife, Ann. Words cannot express the joy that moment brings to me. When I am gone, there is no phone call, no letter, or no fax that can make up the longing I have in my heart to be with her. She feels the same way about me, even after all these years. We have grown closer and closer each and every day.

In Luke, Chapter 15, the father of the prodigal son was longing for his son to come home. There was an emptiness in his heart that no one else could fill but that son. Many times, late at night, he must have said, "Oh, I would give anything if my son would just come home." One day that son returned and repented and was a changed man.

Like the father of Luke 15, God is waiting for someone who is reading this book to return to Him so He can return to them. He desires to be more real to you than you could ever imagine. I thank God for saving me, but there have been many times that He has been more real than my day of salvation. His realness is what changes and keeps on changing our lives. God the Father waits, with open arms, for you. God the Holy Spirit is nudging your heart to motivate you to repent. God, the Son, has paid the price for your fellowship with His very own blood. The price has been paid by Jesus Christ, personally, for your fellowship. Fellowship is much more than eating snacks in the church fellowship hall or at a Sunday School gathering. Fellowship is allowing God to be real, personal, and closer than a brother or a mate in your life. You must open the door. The door is repentance.

Malachi 3:7 says, "Return unto me," which is the one price of repentance. "I will return unto you," is the promise of God, Himself. When God speaks, He is speaking in the present: <u>Now is the time to respond; return to God now, for He is waiting on you.</u>

THREE STEPS TO HEAVEN

"For the Son of man is come to seek and to save that
which is lost." – Luke 19:10

"¹Let not your heart be troubled: ye believe in God, believe also
in me. ²In my Father's house are many mansions: if it were not
so, I would have told you. I go to prepare a place for you. ³And
if I go and prepare a place for you, I will come again, and
receive you unto myself; that where I am, there ye may be also.
⁴And whither I go ye know, and the way ye know."
– John 14:1-4

Doctor Martin Luther of the reformation said, "The Gospel is
a power which saves all who believe it. The Gospel is the divine
Word which is powerful to rescue all who put their trust in it."

My purpose in this chapter is to share the good news of Jesus
Christ, which is God's way to heaven and how to have a right
relationship with Him. I call this the Three Steps to Heaven.
This is how to get right with God.

STEP 1 – UNDERSTAND THE TRUTH ABOUT YOUR OWN HEART

The Bible, which is God's Holy Word, says that we are all
sinners. "For all have sinned, and come short of the glory of
God." (Romans 3:23) And, "As it is written, 'There is none
righteous, no, not one.'" (Romans 3:10) These verses say that

there is no one on earth who does good—no one who does not sin.

You and I were born with a dirty sinful heart. We inherited this from Adam and Eve in the garden of Eden, but we are also sinners by choice. Many times we know what is the right thing to do but we choose to do the wrong thing. Sin is doing anything we know to be wrong in our heart.

For example, it is a sin to curse God or to use His name in vain. It is a sin to have other gods before the one and true God. It is a sin to dishonor (disobey) our parents. It is a sin to hate and murder or to have sex outside of marriage. It is a sin to lie, to cheat, to steal, and so on. (Read the Ten Commandments in the Bible.) There are also attitude sins that we have in our heart. Things like anger, jealousy, bitterness, prejudice, and resentment are sins.

The Bible says we are all guilty sinners before a holy God. Because of our sin, God will not accept us. A couple had two boys who were playing in a muddy stream near their house. They were jumping in and out of the mud splashing one another. When they returned to their house they were covered in mud and stunk like manure.

Their parents would not allow them into their house until they took off their dirty clothes and cleaned up. They were not allowed in the house because they were dirty and smelled bad. If they had come in, they would have brought the mud and foul odor into a clean house.

God's heaven is like a perfect and clean house. He will not allow anyone into His heaven who has a dirty and foul heart. Revelation 21:27 says, "And there shall in no wise enter into it anything that defiles, or causes an abomination or a lie, but only those who are written in the Lamb's Book of Life."

This is the first step to take to get into heaven: to understand that we have a sin problem, a problem with a dirty heart.

STEP 2 – UNDERSTAND THAT JESUS CHRIST PROVIDED AN ANSWER FOR THIS PROBLEM

Luke 19:10 says, "For the Son of man is come to seek and to save that which is lost."

Jesus Christ was born of a virgin. He was the Son of God and yet the Son of man. He was God in the likeness of men. He was the God-man (John 1:1, 14). Jesus lived a perfect life for thirty-three years and though He was tempted like us, He never sinned. He never allowed sin to enter His heart. His whole life was given to helping others, teaching, ministering, healing, and performing miracles.

Some wicked men lied about Him and said He spoke blasphemy against God. They took Him to court, and He was falsely accused and condemned to die by being nailed to a cross—a crucifixion. This was a slow, terrible way to die and was reserved for criminals only, yet Jesus Christ was innocent.

When Jesus was on the cross, all our sins were placed on Him. The Bible says, God made Christ, who knew no sin, to become sin for us (2 Corinthians 5:21). God required sinless, innocent blood to be shed for our sins. Someone had to die to pay for the sins of the world.

Listen to this true story. Many years ago, in Africa, a man had a dream. In the dream he saw the Lord Jesus climbing a high mountain. Jesus was carrying a very heavy load on His back and shoulders. He was struggling to get up the mountain, After some time had passed, the man having the dream asked the Lord a question: "Lord, is that heavy load you are carrying the sins of the world?"

"No," Jesus said, as He slowly turned to the man. He lovingly looked at the man and said, "This heavy load I'm carrying is only your sins."

When Jesus went to the cross, He went there for your sins and mine. He died for you and me. It's not enough to believe Jesus died for the sin of the world. You must believe He died for your sins and mine. We cannot save ourselves. We cannot work our way into heaven by good deeds. If we could work our way into heaven, there would be no need for Jesus to be crucified.

When Jesus died, He was buried in a borrowed tomb. But on the third day He arose from the grave. That's why we have a living Savior. When He arose, he defeated sin, Satan, and death. The resurrected Jesus was seen by His disciples and over 500 witnesses before ascending into heaven to be at the right hand of God. And, as He promised, someday He is coming again to gather all believers.

In **Step 1**, we discovered that we have a dirty, sinful heart. In **Step 2**, Jesus Christ provided a solution to our sinful heart and separation from God. He shed His blood on the cross to pay for our sins. But there is a third step that we must take.

STEP 3 – WE MUST COMMIT OUR LIVES TO CHRIST

When we are young, we tend to think that we will live forever. But the Bible says we will all die someday and after that comes the judgment. Many people are not prepared to die today. You may be one who is not prepared. The truth is that without Christ you're not prepared live or die.

Many of you have no peace inside your heart. People all over the world say they have no peace. Many have no purpose, no meaning, or no direction for living your life. I was that way many years ago, but someone shared the message of Jesus Christ with me. When I heard the message of Christ, I knew I had a dirty, sinful heart. I knew there was something inside of me God would not accept—that something was my sin. I knew that if I died in my sins I would spend an eternity in hell, not heaven.

But I clearly saw and understood that Jesus died on the cross for me—for my sins. In response to this message of Christ, I decided to give my life to Him. I expressed my commitment to Him through a simple prayer. I confessed to Christ that I was a sinner and needed Him to clean up my dirty heart. I said to the Lord Jesus Christ, I turn from my sin and give you my life. I asked Christ to forgive me and come into my heart as my Lord and Savior.

Jesus did several things for me that day:

1.   He came into my life, giving me peace.
2.   He gave me a purpose for living.
3.   He gave me assurance if I were to die tonight, I would go to heaven.

What Jesus did for me He can do for you and everyone that turns from their sin and turns to Jesus for salvation. Revelation 3:20 shows Jesus as knocking on the door of your heart. "If any man hear my voice and open the door, I will come in to him, and will sup with him and he with me."

In just a moment, I will provide you with a sinner's prayer for salvation. But before you read it, please understand that salvation involves more than you simply reading a prayer. Don't read and pray this prayer if you do not mean to give your heart to Jesus. This is a prayer between you and God. The Bible says that "whosoever shall call upon the name of the Lord shall be saved" (Romans 10:13). You are not asking Jesus to be another god inside of you. You must forsake all other gods (idol worship or witchcraft) to receive Jesus. He will not share your heart with anything or anyone else. You must invite Christ into your life to be the Lord—the Master and Savior—of your life.

If you are ready to make a lifelong decision to commit your life to Christ, then say this prayer to God in all sincerity:

"Dear God, I know that I am a sinner and if I died tonight without Jesus, I would spend an eternity in Hell. I now believe that Jesus died on the cross for my sins, was buried, and rose again the third day to save me. I ask Him to come into my life and save me from my sins. Thank you for saving me and giving me the assurance that I am now a child of God and will enter heaven someday. Until then, help me to live every day for Jesus and to help share this message of salvation. In Jesus' name I pray, amen."

If you meant what you just prayed, then listen to what Jesus said just happened to you: "Verily, verily, I say unto you, he that heareth my word and believeth on him (God) that sent me, hath everlasting life, and shall not come into condemnation, but is passed from death unto life" (John 5:24).

THE GOSPEL IN ONE VERSE

"For the wages of sin is death; but the gift of God is eternal life through Jesus Christ our Lord." (Romans 6:23)

This is only one verse, but it is a verse of grave contrasts. It is a contrast of life and death—your life and death! It contrasts your critical condition with God's gift of eternal existence and God's good news of Christ for you. Read further, trusting the Holy Spirit to speak.

Romans 6:23 begins with the words, "For the wages of sin is death..."

I.   FOR THE WAGES – How would you define the term "wages"? Wages are the rewards we receive for working for someone. But what if your "employer" refuses to pay you what you earned? Deep down, you know you deserve getting what is owed to you. God's Word says you are owed a wage—a wage for what?

II.   OF SIN – Underscore the word "sin." This is what you have done toward God for which you deserve a wage. What do you think of when you hear the word, sin? Sin is something everyone has done against God that separates you from Him.

Romans 3:23 says, "For all have sinned and fall short of the glory of God." Sin means to miss the mark. What mark have we missed? This verse says all people have missed the glory of God. It means you and I have failed to give the honor and glory due to God. In other words, we have failed to love Him "with all our heart, with all our soul, and with all our mind." (Matthew 22:37) When God created, He gave man a unique "do this" command in response to creating him: "Hear, O Israel: The Lord our God is one Lord: And thou shalt love the Lord God with all thine heart, and with all thy soul, and with all thy might." (Deuteronomy 6:5)

Jesus said this summed up all the law that God issued (Matthew 22:37-40). But sin caused us to turn away from God's law—His love—and we began loving others and things more than God. Therefore, we have missed the mark—we have failed to give God the honor (love) He deserves from us. We have fallen short of God's law. First John 3:4 says, "Whoever commits sin also commits lawlessness, and sin is lawlessness." We are guilty of violating God's laws by not loving Him first and foremost in our lives.

God's law orders us not to lie: "You shall not bear false witness against your neighbor." (Exodus 20:16) Yet all of us have lied sometime in our lives. How many times do we have to lie to be a liar? Only once!

God's law orders us not to steal, but all of us can recall sometime in our lives when we have stolen. How many times do we have to steal to be called a thief? Only once! We are all idolaters, thieves, and liars. James 2:10-11 says, "For whoever shall keep the whole law, and yet stumble in one point, he is guilty of all. For He who said, 'Do not commit adultery,' also said, 'Do not commit murder.' Now if you do not commit adultery, but you do murder, you have become a transgressor of the law."

We are transgressors of God's law. If you violate the law of your country, you become a criminal. How much greater are you a criminal when you violate the law of God. Romans 3:19 says that all become guilty before God by the law. By His standard—the law—we are all guilty sinners before Him.

III.   IS DEATH – When you think of death, the word separation may enter your thoughts. "Death," in this verse means spiritual separation. Sin has separated you from God, and if you choose to reject God while you are alive, that separation will become an eternal torment in hell. Revelation 21:8 says all idolaters and liars shall have their place in the lake which burns forever with fire and brimstone, which is the second death.

Dying in sin and having rejected God is what you and I earn and deserve as law breakers of His will. This is our earned wage for our sins. However, notice the small but significant next word...

IV.   BUT – This three-letter word is the most important word in the verse because it indicates there is hope for all people. The first phrase of this verse is bad news for all. All are separated from God by their rebellious ways and if they reject Christ, they will spend all of eternity separated from Him in Hell.

But God has good news for us! The Gospel is good news for bad people, and we are bad people because we have transgressed God's law. "But" implies that there is an alternative. Let us turn our attention to God's alternative to the bad news.

V.   THE GIFT – A gift is not earned by the person who receives it. Someone else has paid for it and offers it to you.

How does it make you feel when you are given an expensive gift? Some people feel compelled to do something good for an expensive gift. Likewise, some will try to earn God's favor by doing good deeds, living a moral life, or taking part in religious activities. But it is impossible to earn something that has already been bought and offered to you as a gift.

How would you feel if you had bought an expensive gift for a close friend, but they would not accept it until they paid you for it? If they pay you for it, it no longer is a gift.

VI.   OF GOD – God, who is perfect and holy, wants to give you a gift. It's a gift, not from your best friend, a family member, or a minister, but from God Himself. No one else can offer you this gift but God alone. What is this "gift of God"?

VII.   IS ETERNAL LIFE – "Eternal life" is the opposite of eternal death in Hell. Eternal death is separation from God, but eternal life means being united with God and reconciled with Him forever. (Reconciled means having a favorable relationship reestablished.)

John 17:3 says, "And this is eternal life, that they may know You, the only true God, and Jesus Christ whom You have sent." Eternal life is an intimate love relationship with God forever. Eternal life starts the day you receive the gift and extends into eternity. No one can end it. Jesus said in John 10:28, "And I give them eternal life, and they shall never perish; neither shall anyone (not sin, self, or Satan) snatch them out of my hand." God's gift is eternal life.

VIII.   IN CHRIST JESUS OUR LORD – Jesus is the means through which you obtain the gift of eternal life. John 3:36 says,

"He who believes in the son has everlasting life; and he who does not believe the son shall not see life, but the wrath of God abides on him." Jesus purchased the gift with His own life. No one else has died for your sins. God required innocent blood shed for your sins. The Bible says God made Christ, who knew no sin, to be sin for us, that we might become the righteousness of God in Christ (2 Corinthians 5:21).

Exodus 13:13 says, "But every firstborn of [your beasts] you shall redeem with a lamb; and if you will not redeem it, then you shall break its neck."

Evangelist George Cutting once wrote a story: Imagine we are back in the days of Israel's glory. We are standing in Jerusalem near the Temple. We hear two men talking, one a priest and the other a rich man. Down a narrow street comes a Jewish farmer, leading the foal of a donkey. He approaches the two men.

"Sir," he says to the priest. "This is the firstborn of my animals. Is there any way by which the colt's life may be saved? I am a poor man and I need this animal to help me with my work on my farm."

"Yes," the priest said. "Bring me a lamb and I will offer it in the place of the colt."

"I do not have a lamb."

"Then purchase one with your money and the purchased lamb will be accepted as one raised by you."

The poor farmer looked down at his colt. "I do not have money to purchase a lamb." The farmer raised his moist eyes toward the priest. "Is there no other way?"

The priest shook his head. "This is the law of God; it is explicit and emphatic. If you will not redeem the colt, then you must break its neck."

The rich man listened to the men. "Just a moment," he said to the farmer and priest. Then he turned to the farmer. "In my home, I have a spotless, pet lamb. I will hurry home and bring it to you so that you may offer it instead of your colt."

"But I cannot pay you for it," the farmer responded.

The rich man smiled. "It's not for sale; it is my gift to you."

The rich man hurried home, retrieved his pet lamb, and brought it to the farmer, who offered it to the priest. The priest bound the lamb and slit its throat, shedding its blood.

Can the priest now demand that the colt's neck be broken? No. Its life has been redeemed by the death of the lamb. Now the farmer can return home rejoicing that his colt has been spared. That story explains God's plan of salvation. To redeem us from the penalty of our sins, God offered up His own Son as "the lamb of God, which taketh away the sin of the world." (John 1:29)

CONCLUSION – If I offered you an expensive ink pen that I bought with my own money, as a gift to you, at what point does the pen become yours? It becomes yours when you reach out your hand and take it from me. While the pen is in my possession, it is not yours to enjoy.

You have a choice to make. God is offering His only begotten Son to you as a substitute offering for the penalty of your sins. You can reject His offer of Jesus Christ or you can receive Him. The choice is yours to make right now. The question is, will you receive Christ into your life?

HOW TO RECEIVE CHRIST

1. **Confess** – Agree with God that you are a sinner that deserves death and Hell.

2. **Surrender** – Commit your whole life to Christ, to please Him and not yourself. Make Christ the final authority (Lord) of your life. Surrender the throne of your heart to His Lordship.

When a person confesses and surrenders his life to Christ, that person passes from death to life. The wages for our sins is death, but the gift of God is eternal life in Christ Jesus our Lord. When you receive Christ, the Bible says you become "a new creature: old things are passed away; behold, all things become new" (2 Corinthians 5:17).

AN EXAMPLE PRAYER – Use this prayer as a guide to receive God's plan for your salvation:

"Dear God, I agree with You that I am a guilty sinner who deserves Your wrath for my sins. I confess my sins and my need for a Savior. I believe Your only begotten Son, Jesus, is the Christ who paid the penalty for my sins. I, by faith, receive Jesus into my life to save me from eternal separation from You and to give me the gift of eternal life. Thank You for saving me and making me a new creature in Christ Jesus. Amen."

FROM ME TO YOU

"THE THRILL IS GONE" is the title of a song that recording artist B. B. King sang a few years ago. This song title sums up the lives on many people today.

The thrill may be gone from your life. Many people just exist instead of live. They have no purpose or direction in life.

You may be a success in school, business, or in your social life, but inside you know that something is missing. You know there has to be more to life than what you have.

Leroy Hassler preaching in 1975.

God has given me a genuine purpose in life. Jesus Christ has become the Lord of my life. I came to realize I had fallen short of God's plan for my life. At my invitation, Jesus Christ came into my life. He became my personal Savior. I knew if I died, I would go to heaven. Christ makes my daily life far more meaningful also.

115

This same Jesus that I love so much died for your failures, sorrows, and sins. He was nailed to a cross. Spikes were driven through His sinless hands and blood-soaked Roman cross for our sins. He died and was buried but rose out of the grave. He defeated death.

God gave His best for you and me. "For God so loved the world, that He gave is only begotten Son, that whosoever believeth in Him should not perish, but have everlasting life." John 3:16

Living for Christ is not the most popular way of life, but it is the most joyous I have ever known.

I challenge you to pray and invite Jesus Christ into your life. The Bible says in Romans 10:13 "For whosoever shall call upon the name of the Lord shall be saved."

If you are willing to begin a new life, I invite you to commit your life to Jesus Christ by faith. I invite you to pray this prayer:

Dear God, I know that I have sinned. I know that I have fallen short of Your plan for my life. I believe that Jesus Christ died and rose again so that I could have a new life. Dear Jesus, forgive me and take control of my life. I am sorry that I have lived this long without You. Thank You for dying for my sins. Please help me to live for You. In Jesus Name, Amen. *

*Leroy Hassler wrote the above for a tract in about 1975.

RANDALL JINKINS by Leroy Hassler

One of the greatest blessings of our lives was going to Eastside Baptist Church at Rusk, Texas to be the pastor in February of 1983. I did a lot of personal visitations both to church members and to the lost. My wife went with me on a lot of these visits.

Randall Jinkins and Leroy Hassler

One thing I found out quickly was on such a large church field that I needed local help to find the people and their homes. Some of them lived as far as 35 miles away from the church. Randall Jinkins volunteered a lot of his time helping me find

117

people and making these visits with me. I never could thank him enough for his help. This took a lot of time, but it was time well spent with some people getting back in church and some making professions of faith in Christ. Randall and his wife Tracy were a great blessing to us and to our church. It has been a long time now, but we think Randall was the first deacon the church ordained while I was the pastor there.

I remember Randall telling about going to Kenya with First Baptist Church in Euless, Texas. As Randall talked about the thousands of people that came to Christ on that trip it was more than I could comprehend. I did not know it then, that I would be telling people about vast numbers of people coming to Christ on the mission trips we made and knowing that many of the people who heard about it had no frame of reference. In fact, I ended up going to some of the same places Randall had done ministry in.

Randall has made numerous trips with Hassler Evangelistic Ministries and has done an excellent job, but that is always true about Randall's work for our Lord. Randall is working with his own ministry now and doing a great job.

This chapter will be near the end of this book but maybe it should have been near the front. Many people helped me, as I was a pastor at Rusk. If I started naming names, I would probably leave some out, so I better stop here. Randall and his wife Tracy still live at Rusk, Texas. Brother Randall is now the pastor of Hilltop Baptist Church in Frankston, Texas.

BROTHER HENRY JOHNSON 1935 – 2018

Brother Henry,

We rejoice that in 1973 God caused our paths in life to cross at Dothan, Alabama. Our time at Cloverdale Baptist Church under your ministry was not only life changing it was as close to heaven as we may be upon this earth. Ann and I both grew spiritually and had a measure of personal revival that no doubt is where our present ministry started. We both gained a burden for souls, revival, and world evangelism. We started praying for those things, not knowing our ministry would in the future reach millions of people for Christ. We deserve no credit, nor will we take any as we say often, All Glory to God!

While at Cloverdale I learned much from you about the local church and how to be an effective pastor, at the time I did not know I would someday pastor a church. I learned how to witness and win people to Christ from you. I still remember parts of some of the messages you preached at Cloverdale. We both learned from every revival meeting, January Bible study, and special event at Cloverdale. In fact, I still can repeat some of a message Wesley Willis preached at Cloverdale, with the title "Trust and Obey."

We were both impressed greatly by God with the life you lived in front of us. You were a great example for us to follow. Not many days go by that you are not in our thoughts and our conversation. We will always look toward and up to you. Your advice has been counted on many times and has proved accurate and helpful.

Our time with you and your family was valuable and wonderful, that includes Gaius. We pray for him and his family regularly. We know we cannot live in the past, but it is good to remember a great past under your ministry and being your friend.

Sincerely, Leroy and Ann Hassler

Brother Henry passed away in 2018. He left behind his wonderful wife, Sarah, his son, Gaius, and his wife, and grandchildren. This letter was written by Leroy to commemorate Brother Henry's 81st birthday.

OTHER BOOKS BY LEROY HASSLER

CONTENTS:

Introduction: In Search of a Man
The Kind of Preacher God Can Use in
God-sent Revival...

1 - ...Will Be a Holy Man of God
2 - ...Will Be a Man of Prayer
3 - ...Will Be a Man of the Word
4 - ...Will Hate Sin
5 - ...Will Love God and Love Souls
6 - ...Will Lead His Local Church to
    Pursue Genuine Revival
7 - What You Can Do To Be the Kind of
    Preacher That God Can Use in
    God-sent Revival
8 - What You can Do To Help Your
    Pastor Be the Kind of Preacher
    God Can Use in God-sent Revival
9 - What You Can Do As a Church Member To Help Bring God-
    sent Revival To Your Local Church
Postscript—The Great Commission and God-sent Revival

ORDER INFORMATION: www.hasslerministries.com
(Look under "Resources" tab)

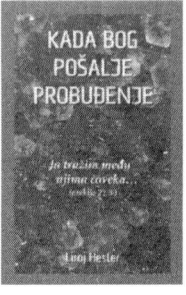

Leroy's first book published
in the Serbian Language!

GO! Obeying God in World Evangelism and Revival

Leroy's second book describing his call to lead over 2 million people to Christ on all the world's continents.

"The story that unfolds in these pages will astonish you and challenge you... I have never known a man with more genuine humility than Leroy Hassler."
– James T. Draper, President Emeritus, LifeWay Christian Resources

ISBN: 978-0-9825827-0-1

ORDER INFORMATION: www.hasslerministries.com
(Look under "Resources" tab)

HASSLER EVANGELISTIC MINISTRIES, INC.
P. O. Box 1791
Gladewater, Texas 75647 USA

ABOUT THE AUTHOR

Leroy Hassler has been preaching the gospel since 1974. For nearly 4 years he was the pastor of Eastside Baptist Church of Rusk, Texas. God allowed him to see every attendance record broken. As a vocational evangelist his ministry has crossed the U.S.A. from Maryland to Florida and from Ohio to New Mexico. He has preached the gospel over 1,250 times on six continents. He has preached in over 600 churches. His ministry has helped start over 400 new churches, many of them in Africa. The ministry has given away thousands of Bibles in China and Africa and fed thousands of hungry people in Africa.

For seventeen consecutive years the ministry has reached over 100,000 people a year. Over four million people have made professions of faith in Christ and probably many more.

Leroy is a lifetime member of Ring 10 Veteran Boxers Association, New York City, NY.

Leroy's wife, Ann, is the office manager for their ministries in America. They live in East Texas and are members of Mobberly Baptist Church in Longview, Texas.